DISMANTLING
THE STRUCTURE OF
THE
EGO

Also by Jacqui Derbecker

Books

Movement of Stillness - As Revealed in the New Mayan Calendar – Post 2012
(Bloomington, USA. Balboa Publishing,
A Division of Hay House. 2011.).

Movement of Stillness reveals the new Mayan Calendar, post-2012, as well as one hundred prophecies called "All Truths." Through the process of automatic writing Jacqui Derbecker felt honoured to channel Edgar Cayce. Cayce was a well-known mystic philosopher, channeler and author (1877 – 1945). Each "All Truth" touches upon all aspects of everyday living as we learn to move into stillness.

balboapress.com
chapters.com
amazon.com

barnesandnoble.com
jacquiconsults.com
thewaterviewspace.com

Card Decks

Know, Allow, Believe Cards
(The Waterview Space Publishing. Ontario, Canada. 2011.).

www.jacquiconsults.com
www.thewaterviewspace.com

These empowering eighty cards provide messages that will assist you in:

- **Knowing** and recognizing your true self.
- **Allowing** your truth to shine forth.
- **Believing** in yourself.

Blockages will be released, limiting thoughts and emotional patterns will be dismantled as you read and allow the cards' messages to be absorbed. These cards were channeled from a large collective Soul Entity named **Abraham**, whose messages are filled with love and peace.

DISMANTLING
THE STRUCTURE OF
THE
EGO

RESTRUCTURING EVERYTHING BUILD UPON EGO

- ***Realizing*** ego is illusion.

- ***Recognizing*** there is no longer a ***now*** moment and how this is possible?

- ***Reconfiguration*** of the Law of Attraction.

Jacqui Derbecker

BALBOA
PRESS

A DIVISION OF HAY HOUSE

Balboa Press books may be ordered through booksellers or by contacting:

Balboa Press
A Division of Hay House
1663 Liberty Drive
Bloomington, IN 47403
www.balboapress.com
1-(877) 407-4847

Because of the dynamic nature of the Internet, any web addresses or links contained in this book may have changed since publication and may no longer be valid. The views expressed in this work are solely those of the author and do not necessarily reflect the views of the publisher, and the publisher hereby disclaims any responsibility for them.

The author of this book does not dispense medical advice or prescribe the use of any technique as a form of treatment for physical, emotional, or medical problems without the advice of a physician, either directly or indirectly. The intent of the author is only to offer information of a general nature to help you in your quest for emotional and spiritual well-being. In the event you use any of the information in this book for yourself, which is your constitutional right, the author and the publisher assume no responsibility for your actions.

Any people depicted in stock imagery provided by Thinkstock are models, and such images are being used for illustrative purposes only.
Certain stock imagery © Thinkstock.

Printed in the United States of America

ISBN: 978-1-4525-6625-2 (sc)
ISBN: 978-1-4525-6626-9 (e)

Balboa Press rev. date: 2/14/2013

"Real love is what you are born with. Real love is what you are."

Don Miguel Ruiz
(Toltec master)

"No matter where I am, there is only infinite good, infinite wisdom, infinite harmony and infinite love."

Dr. Wayne Dyer
(spiritual teacher)

"We become what we think about all day long."

Ralph Waldo Emerson
(author)

"Feeling grateful to or appreciative of someone or something actually attracts more of the things that you appreciate and value in your life."

Christine Northup
(medical doctor and women's wellness expert)

"Surely joy is the condition of life."

Henry David Thoreau
(philosopher)

"If you peel back the layers of your life – the frenzy, the noise, stillness is waiting. That stillness is you."

Oprah

Gifted To ...

The *stillness* of
who you are All Ready.

Contents

An Acknowledgement

Acknowledge that you are living through an amazing era as new wonderful energies continue to emerge upon the planet and enter into all facets of our lives. We are being shifted and restructured back to our Original Self through the beauty of love. It is time to embrace these new energies and flow with this universal transition.

Thank You

It is with great joy that I wish to give thanks and love to Spirit – to All – to the Oneness. For the kindness and support of my favourite Tea Room families. Thank you John Teffer for your kindness and most generous contribution, and the timeless typing of Shannon Chan. To the wonderful Mary Ellen Koroscil for your unending editing and advice. Blessings to the Balboa Press team for your guidance. A special thank you to Cheryl McCague-Shane, Marly Freer, Suzanne Dobinson, Jill Strapp, Lona McBoyle and Jocelyn Griffiths. Hugs to all of the evening participants at The Waterview Space. Acknowledgements and thanks to the voices and wisdom of those great teachers quoted herein. I am grateful.

Part 1

The Beginning

*You are Spirit within a coat called human,
similar to how a tiny blade of grass is Spirit
covered in a little jacket of green.*

Introduction

The way in which you participate in life is determined by love and nothing else.

This book is dedicated to assisting you in shifting your awareness into:

- *Realizing* that you are Spirit and love.
- *Rejuvenating* your life through a true awareness of self.
- *Restructuring* everything and anything that was built upon ego.
- *Releasing* and living only from ease and nothing more.

It is during these times of awakening, you will experience the recognition, exposure and the dismantling and dissolving of the ego in all areas of your life. It is a time of releasing and awakening to your true still self, the one who is only love and lives from this love.

As the words in this book streamed or channeled through me I felt a most powerful loving force, a feeling of energy being emitted from my pen within the words that fell onto my paper. I have been engaged in a process of what is described as *automatic writing*, whereby messages move through me via my handwriting. This began for me several years ago on my thirty-seventh birthday. I was writing in my journal and all at once felt a warmth expand from inside of me and near me. I then began to write but without any effort or thinking. The feelings were peace*full*, joy*full* and a knowing that I was a vessel for the messages to move through me from Spirit.

My first book entitled *"Movement of Stillness – As Revealed in the New Mayan Calendar – Post 2012"* (*Movement of Stillness*. Bloomington, USA. Balboa Publishing, A Division of Hay House. 2012.) is composed of channeled messages from Edgar Cayce (1877-1945). Cayce was a well-known mystic philosopher and medical intuitive who was regarded as the one who connected the body, mind, and soul to healing. He was a respected channeler, seer and medium, and it was a great honour for me to channel his messages. These messages within my book *Movement of Stillness* speak to about one-hundred **All Truths** or prophecies which touch upon the daily living aspects of career, emotion, finance, physical body, mind, Spirit, community and relationships.

Each **All Truth** describes the unfoldment or the remembering of your true self, which is love. One **All Truth** is the dismantling and dissolving of the ego, which will be explained in detail within the pages of this book. Some incredible "reveal"ations will be exposed about ego and its end upon the planet. It is time to really know that you truly are living during some profound times.

I invite you to read and feel the language of the messages as a channeled gift to you. These messages upon the pages of this book are gently arranged and tenderly placed. Explore into **your self** as you read more deeply into these pages. Allow this book to **read you** and help you to recognize where in your life ego beliefs are being dismantled. You may feel a gentle releasing or dismantling of ego based thoughts, behavior patterns, stories, emotions and opinions. Just allow this releasing to occur by loosening the hold of ego beliefs and flow into a **Lightness of Being** or a **freeing**. You know you are free when you no longer need to pretend to be someone you are not.

You will notice that some of the words channeled through me have reorganized their spelling and form in order to enrich the messages' meaning. For example, the word *yourself* has been shifted into two words *your* and *self*, bringing an emphasis to self. Also repetition of certain words and phrases is staged purposefully in order to bring forth positive feelings and to generate ideas which are woven within the pages of this book.

As you read, simply allow the Spirit of truth to reform your being into that of Oneness which is filled with love and peace or a *silent beingness*, which is a deep nourishment of self. It is intertwined amongst the silentness that reveals your precious being. The dismantling of the ego is allowing you to arrive in those silent spaces or gaps and it is here you discover this precious still state of beingness. As you loosen the hold of ego beliefs more silent spaces will open up for you. You then begin to feel a silence not only in *your self* but within the stillness streaming through the beams designed by the moon, the dew drop loving kisses, the movement of wind through the quiet trees as they stand awaiting for their massage and caress of the earth's breath or wind. It is through the *eurhythmics* of this silent rhythm where you discover life and love.

When you place yourself within the arms of who you truly are you accept all that begins and ends with you, which is grace, nothing more. All spaces are grace-filled – you just need to allow this to happen. This is aptly versed in the poem *Song of Life* by poet John Teffer.

Song of Life

It's the music you play.
It's the art you paint.
It's the words you say.
It's the part you play.
It's the script you write.
It's the ending you choose or the beginning you start and
most importantly it's the space inbetween that you fill.

It is now time for you to sing your song of ***silent beingness*** which originates from a place of love that really has no language, as you will discover reading this glorious book.

Beginning

This powerful, yet gentle book, *Dismantling the Structure of the Ego* will focus upon recognizing yourself from the perspective of being Spirit and living from that Source, therefore dismantling the ego. You may believe conceptually that ego and Spirit have historically co-existed together to form your identity. Spirit or Essence on one side and ego occupies the other side. This concept has been explained theoretically by many great thinkers, philosophers and theorists with ego defined as the foundation of personality governed by id or superego. It has been left open to a plethora of interpretations and explanations all depending on one's personal preference.

I invite you to explore your current understanding of ego throughout these next number of pages. The concept of ego or Edging Grace Out will be examined thoroughly and then defined from a different perspective. What will be revealed to you is how the ego is being dismantled and dissolving piece by piece over the next number of years and in fact this has already started.

Ego is illusion, it can no longer hold the structure of itself as truth anymore. It is destroying people, plants, animals, sea creatures, all life forms. The structure of the ego carries with it pain, fear, suffering, destruction of self and others through wars, jealousy, abuse, torture and lies. The concept of believing the teachings of the ego has allowed the creation of a false identity for humanity which collectively has resulted in destruction, killings and war, with a movement away from love. When you are feeling unsafe or unloved within yourself you then begin to create fear, pain and suffering.

Within this book are messages where you will discover a peace*full*ness and a movement of stillness, which encourages you to walk and rest as stillness. In other words, you are stillness in movement similar to a walking peace-filled mantra or prayer, devoid of any suffering needs, pain and anger. Now is a time to reflect upon your life and the situations in your life that possibly define who and what you think or feel you are. Perhaps you are just simply love, nothing more and this is the only truth. You were born from love and only from love. Were you actually born as hatred? Of course not! It is time to come forth with your truth and nothing more than your truth. You are truth, you are Source, you are only love.

During this Time of Transparency and The Age of Aquarius you will witness the dismantling of everything that has been built upon ego. Everything that was and is structured around ego is now being taken apart, piece by piece and then the dissolving of every single falsity occurs. Within this dissolving of these dismantled pieces is the exposure of the White Light where one finds their joy, peace, happiness and all that is their true self. You will be aware that life and living life is all about love and only living from love – nothing more than this. You will discover that love emanates from you like the light streaming from the sun.

In the first few chapters of this book you will learn about further explanations of the ego as related to illusion. Read deeply into these pages and feel an unfolding of truth and grace within yourself. A truth which you already know but just couldn't explain nor understand. As you read these passages notice there are several ego structures being dismantled. This is just a sprinkle or a sampling of what is occurring upon the planet during these unique times of shifting and transitioning into your complete being of Oneness. It is a recognition that you are **All Ready** love and One with The Being or Source/God/White Light. It really doesn't matter what term you use to bring language to the energy of The One – The Creator – The One of 1000 names – The Nameless – The Invisible Star Nations – God – White Light.

When you tenderly dive into the following pages of words within this book *feel* what is going on inside of you. Ask yourself, "What am I observing and thinking?" Be aware and ready to explore the concept and origination of ego through The Ego Curriculum and Questions, The "R" Points of Existence, The Now Curriculum and Questions and the diagrams of the dismantling of ego.

Be open and just allow.

What is Ego?

The ego is tied to a false belief system which stems from an institutional or theoretical ideology that was created by theorists/psychologists as a premise to explain pain, suffering, greed and fear. Fear actually means and reflects *f*alse *e*xpectations *a*ppearing *r*eal or *f*orgetting *e*verything is *a*ll *r*ight or *f*orgetting *e*verything is *a*ll *r*eady. However, during the time in history when ego, super ego and id were labelled, the idea of fear was perceived as being very real and in some cases encouraged, as it still seems to be today. For example, the fear of being attacked by another country or person. On a personal basis the fear of not being good enough, young enough, smart enough or the fear of not being able to get the job done or project accomplished, and the list goes on and on. However, people are now beginning to recognize that fear, worry, anxiety or stress is no longer needed and doesn't identify with who you truly are. Therefore can we conclude that ego is an illusion?

No matter what the context(s) are of ego, it is actually the absence of love. In other words, when you feel and live as love there is no fear or ego. Ego can't equate with love, it doesn't have this high vibration or frequency nor does it recognize love or Spirit. Love has a high vibration or energy which vibrates at a very fine level. You may wish to read David Hawkins book *Power vs. Force* (Hawkins, David. *Power vs. Force*. Sedona, Arizona. Veritas Publishing. 1998.) and his interpretation of energy vibration. Through kinesiology, Hawkins devised a clear and consistent scale that calibrated a numerical energy range according to all forms of human expression. Emotions, perceptions, attitudes, world views and spiritual beliefs were assigned numerical values or energy levels from 1 to 1000 based on consistent well documented test results. Our body's muscles clearly respond to the energetic vibration of words, feelings or concepts. For example, the calibrated energy vibration for love is 500, and joy 540, isness which is higher than bliss calibrates as 1000. The higher the number or level your energy vibrates the more love you are living. If you are living or your energy level is vibrating at 800 this means you have let go of blame, hurt, pain, guilt and other pain-filled emotions which energetically vibrate at a lower, heavy, sluggish rate of 20-150. To live from the ***feeling*** of love indicates you are living in the present now moment.

Emotion means believing the old story of your childhood memories of hurt and pain. Perhaps you are sixty-five years old and still re-living your old childhood beliefs of abandonment, abuse, or alcoholic parents which happened when you were five years old. So now you live by these triggers even though this occurred sixty years ago. It is imperative that you loosen the hold of the old story and beliefs. Move ahead into a person who is a grown-up mature adult and lives as who you truly are, which is a being comprised of Light and Love. When you begin to recognize this, you begin to live and see life as it truly is, which is just love and joy. The ego wants you to hang onto the old story and continue to wallow around in its pain. This triggers not only emotional pain but physical pain as well which builds and creates more of the same pain.

Why would you choose to live with this type of pain? You may say to yourself, "Well my father abused me and look how my patterns of relationships have only been with men who have been abusive?" Or, "I feel abandoned and lonely all the time because I was placed in ten different foster homes, so I will always feel a sense of abandonment." These are just two of hundreds of examples of the pain of emotions attached to an old story or belief. Do you see how victimized one can become? Allowing victimization to continue to grow at an adult age is no longer acceptable. You must recognize and realize that there is only the purity of love. Now is a time on this planet to become filled with realizations and recognitions that all is **wonderful** and **filled with wonder**. All is within the absolute Divine plan.

There is nothing out of step, everything is synchronized perfectly. Begin today to realize and to recognize this to be true. Ego is just simply thoughts of destruction and pain and these thoughts may not even be your own but someone else's thoughts. You are believing these to be true because of the programmed beliefs from parents, family and society. The ego wants to use these thoughts to create anxiety, confusion, fear, anger, pain and all forms of suffering. These thoughts then become habit and you begin to forget who you truly are, which is just love.

Perhaps the term ego is no longer to be applied since even labelling it provides it a definition, an identity, a form of language that gives a perceived sense of power or creation. Perhaps the terms **e**dging **g**race **o**ut or **e**dging **G**od **o**ut are more appropriate to use and even so we are just re-defining something that we, as people or Spirits in human form are saying doesn't exist anymore. Ego can no longer get a hold of your mind. This means **no more** wars, abuse, torture, hatred, worthlessness, self-sabotage, greed and envy. When you declare, "I am no longer living this way of suffering anymore," then you won't and you reprogram your mind and your thought patterns into thoughts of beauty, love, passion, compassion, empathy and peace. You no longer live through anxiety and fear. You no longer remain attached to the old emotional story from childhood and are able to let this go because you know who you truly are, a being of **love**.

You surrender and let go into the softness of life. As more individuals recognize they no longer need to believe ego you will see them softening as their recognition of love increases.

The Origin of Ego

Where did ego originate from? Where did Freud (1856 – 1939) and others discover ego and why did they label it? To label it, it had to be there in the first place. In the book *Past and Present* (Carlyle, Thomas. *Past and Present*. London, UK. Oxford University Press. 1915.) the author refers to a statement made by a psychiatrist/psychologist, other than Freud, in 1934 at a dinner for the "Friends of the Sigmund Freud Society." After his comments he was banned from the society and moved away to grow vegetables. He said, "Did any of you ever think that along about the time that a notion of a soul gave out Freud popped up with the ego to take its place? The timing of the man! Did he pause to reflect? Irresponsible old coot! It is my belief that men must spout this twaddle about egos, because they fear they have no soul! Think upon it!" Indeed this was a wonderful statement and injected during a time when ego was labelled, studied and even honoured. The man had such courage and honesty to speak truth.

The Biblical interpretation of the origin of ego indicates that ego was a choice. For example, the Christian Biblical reference occurs in the Garden of Eden when Eve is approached by a snake presenting her with a shiny red apple. Paraphrasing, the snake says, "If you eat this apple from the Tree of Knowledge you will be given the knowledge of good and evil." What is her choice? What does she want? She wants wisdom and knowledge, thus ego. The ego perception is that the more wisdom and knowledge one has the more perceived power you own.

What if the story changed and Eve were living from a place free of a need to be wise. She would say to the ego snake, "Gotcha ego, no thank-you, I know who I am now. I am grace."

The ego snake would then slither away into its hole. You see how the Garden of Eden, the apple, the snake symbolizes Spirit and ego. Another example of ego as a form of choice is told in the Story analogy of Two Wolves. As you read the below Story of Two Wolves ask yourself, "Is there a choice?"

A STORY OF TWO WOLVES

An old Cherokee is teaching his grandson about life.
"A fight is going on inside me," he said to the
boy. "It is a terrible fight and it is
between two wolves. One is evil – he is anger,
envy, sorrow, regret, greed, arrogance,
self-pity, guilt, resentment, inferiority, lies,
false pride, superiority, and ego."
He continued, "The other is good – he is joy,
peace, love, hope, serenity, humility,
kindness, benevolence, empathy, generosity, truth,
compassion, and faith. The same fight
is going on inside you – and inside every other person, too."
The grandson thought about it for a minute
and then asked his grandfather,
"Which wolf will win?"
The old Cherokee simply replied, "The one you feed."

- Anonymous

Which one do you feed? In other words, which one is real to you? The one you believe in the most is the one you will feed. The one that is truly you is the only one to feed and it is joy, peace, love and compassion. Why would you choose to live a life of pain, suffering and sabotage? There really is no choice because if you live from truth you feed or attract more joy, peace and love back into your life. That is all there is and everything else is illusion and false.

So then where did ego come from? Is there an answer? Some would believe ego is the term used for the opposite of love or moving in the other direction of love – but where did this other direction come from? Is ego demonic, evil and hatred? The message about this is wrapped around our English language and all languages. It is important to feel, see and be aware of how language intertwines itself around these terms relating to ego. Ego is simply not love. But where did this ***not love*** come from? God? Source? White Light? After all, isn't God, Source, White Light, love and only love? If this is the case why would ego, which means pain, originate from God? Is it a test? Is it punishment? Is it karma that you believe needs to be cleared out in our lifetime? If all people are God or White Light then why would God or you allow ego to enter into the equation?

Much interest has been created and these questions are now being explored further. However, the origination of ego is not being revealed at this time upon the planet. A point of ***amnesia*** exists, regardless how deeply you are able to explore, seek or transmit information from spiritual sources or study certain ancient, sacred, text books. You will never discover the origins of ego. Certainly you may wish to delve back into historical accounts of early life, however, the ego goes back further than this and there is actually an ***energy blockage*** or a ***no revealing*** of the origins of ego. Which simply means it will not be revealed at this time, much like these other points of amnesia or energy blockages of information as listed below:

Points of Amnesia or Energy Blockages

1. You will not discover how the human body came into existence.

2. You will not discover how the universe was created.

3. You will not discover what truly happened to the dinosaur age. This will never be discovered in its truest form.

4. You will not discover or remember how your Spirit was released from The Being in order to manifest into your human form.

5. You will not know or discover the origins of ego as this information has also been energetically blocked.

6. When you move completely into the Homo-Luminous form from the human heavy matter form, you will never remember the transition or the metamorphosis from the human form into the Homo-Luminous form. What exactly is the Homo-Luminous form? All people are slowly sliding into the new way of existing or living called the Homo-Luminous way of existing. The Homo-Sapiens way of living is the human form that relates to the hunter/gatherer. The Homo-Luminous form of living is one of pure Light and the full realization that you are Light. This is actually not a form but only Light – one of trust, passion, peace, love and grace. There will be no human body form when we are the fullest of the Homo-Luminous. We will just simply be White Light.

The Homo-Luminous is beautifully illustrated in *Sacred Mirrors* a 1990 book by Alex Grey (Grey, Alex. *Sacred Mirrors: The Visionary Art of Alexander Grey*. Rochester, Vermont. Inner Traditions International. 1990). He illustrates how the human form is melding into the White Light Spirit formlessness or Homo-Luminous creating the purity of Spirit only. His book is filled with channeled illustrations supporting the spiritual transformation or ascension. The spiritual evolution is slowly sliding us back to its Original Oneness with Spirit. Therefore when we arrive as Homo-Luminous we will not remember the human body form, thus a point of amnesia. This transition from human form to the Homo-Luminous may take hundreds of years (see the Glossary for further explanations of the Homo-Luminous form and Homo-Sapien form).

Another block that is presently evolving is a blockage of information or intellectual knowledge. In other words, as individuals move into trying to reason and figure everything out, the more the information will back away from them. People are investigating, studying, researching everything for purpose of power, greed and money; this is ego and *this* way of information gathering will not be given because it is ego based. Feelings, rather than thinking or intellectualizing, are emerging and making themselves deeply known.

Allow yourself to feel more and think less, for this is the time of the evolution of Spirit. To practice and embrace your feelings simply walk in the forest and *feel* the vibration and energy of a bird instead of calculating its name and the intellectual concepts wrapped around its existence. Just listen to its song, observe its body and stillness. It is now time to no longer turn to the page in your bird watcher book to seek information about the bird, but to feel its essence instead and truly listen to its song and message of verse between its bar of tones.

View the illustration of the *Ascension Process* (Figure 1) beginning with the creation of ego and the evolution through ego. As we evolve through ego, it needs to be *exposed* and then *recognized* that it is illusion, then the *dismantling* and *dissolving* will occur. The core of all people's existence is love and love does not want to injure or hurt anyone, whereas ego does. When one reaches this place of exposure the dismantling occurs, followed by an inner most awakening. There is also a thinning of the human body veil and finally an illuminated Light, where the weightless self is revealed.

As you examine the Ascension Process (Figure 1), note the Homo-Luminous at the top of this Figure of the Ascension Process. It is free of fear, free of any form of ego illusion – just freedom. Observe how each unfolding step or slide of the Ascension Process shifts into the next step or slide. This begins with the solid foundation as formed by Spirit holding the structure in place for the ascension. Spirit is *always* here in *all ways*, remember that you are Spirit already.

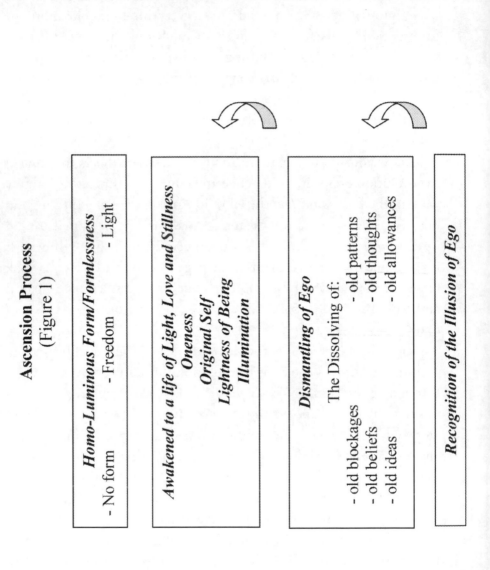

Ascension Process
(Figure 1)

Homo-Luminous Form/Formlessness

- No form   - Freedom   - Light

Awakened to a life of Light, Love and Stillness
Oneness
Original Self
Lightness of Being
Illumination

Dismantling of Ego

The Dissolving of:

- old blockages
- old beliefs
- old ideas
- old patterns
- old thoughts
- old allowances

Recognition of the Illusion of Ego

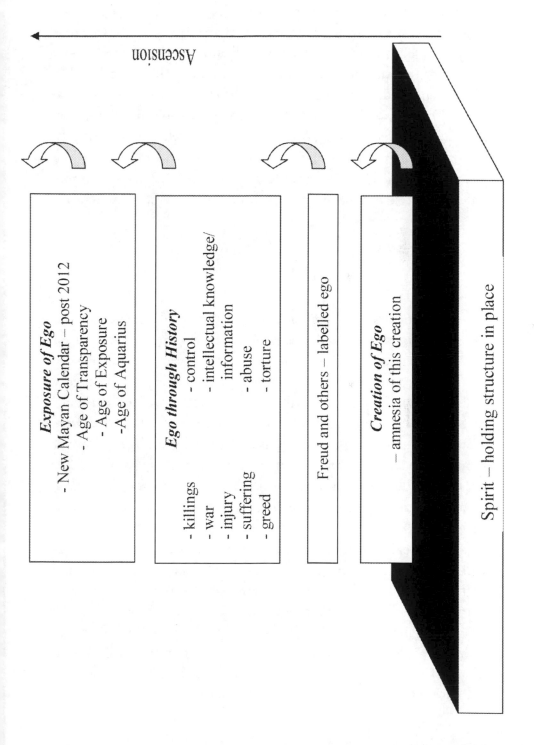

Ascension

Exposure of Ego
- New Mayan Calendar – post 2012
- Age of Transparency
- Age of Exposure
- Age of Aquarius

Ego through History
- control
- intellectual knowledge/ information
- abuse
- torture
- killings
- war
- injury
- suffering
- greed

Freud and others – labelled ego

Creation of Ego
– amnesia of this creation

Spirit – holding structure in place

The soul/sole purpose of ego dismantling is to bring people **back to grace**. We are returning back to the Original Being, to the Oneness of all people, to where you once came from. It is time to step aside, get out of the way and realize that all are One with each other. My other channeled book entitled *"Movement of Stillness – As Revealed in the New Mayan Calendar – Post 2012"* speaks volumes about how we are shifting, as a planet, back to Oneness of self or your true self. It is a time to recognize this shift is happening as revealed in the visual design of the new Mayan Calendar post 2012. This is simply an empty circle or Oneness of Self through the Crystals existence.

The emptiness of the circle indicates no words, no scripts, no diagrams, just vastness with crystal energies. This means each person has the energy of crystals within their water molecules. Water is the main component of your body and this crystal energy is the energy which carries the messages of love and the **All Truths** of existence to the core of who you are or your authentic self. The **All Truths** are within each and every one of us and they depict the new way of living which stems from your authentic true self. There are about 100 **All Truths** described in detail in my book *Movement of Stillness*. I would encourage you to read these and feel the messages embedded in each word.

As you can see, it is a time for revelations and revealing that which is truth. This is the end of the Age of Reason, Industrialization and Intellect. It is the **Age of Transparency** (openness, exposure) and it is also the **Age of Aquarius** (water, flow). The lyrics in the song *Aquarius* from the 1970's expresses this Age as time of crystal messages or revelations being revealed, and the mind's true liberation or an opening to freedom. The lyrics capture the essence of what is presently naturally occurring upon the planet.

Aquarius

"This is the dawning of the age of Aquarius ...
Harmony and understanding ...
Mystic crystal revelation ...
And the minds true liberation ..."

(Ragni, Gerome; Rado, James and MacDermon,
Galt. *Age of Aquarius*. New York, US. The 5th
Dimension, Arista Records. 1972.)

The information carried through the crystals or crystal's energy is considered to be messages of love, peace, joy, passion and compassion and is not based on information to feed ego. This is a time when people will begin to ask questions: "What is my soul's purpose?" "Who am I?" "What is my passion?" It is a time to switch your thoughts to love and only love, then you begin to realize there are actually **no thoughts**, only feelings of pure love and in fact no more questions will present themselves. You are simply reflecting the light of love from within your self to others.

Ego encourages self-loathing, self-serving thoughts, disrespect of self with no dignity; all of which are the illusory snares of the ego. Declare yourself as sacred, surrender and move into the place of stillness where ego beliefs cannot survive. Walk over the threshold into this place of stillness and live as you are **All Ready**. It is a place where you empty everything out and rid yourself of the baggage of old beliefs and ideas. When here you will live in a ready designed sacred structure of loving boldly, being in complete love, harmony, and living as peace. If you are not at peace with **your self**, you are at peace with nothing.

When experiencing peace and harmony you hear and feel nature's music. You begin to realize that the vibration of the sun gifts the songbirds with their musical charms and that the forest is endless or never ending, vast and filled with beauty. You begin to notice nature's details like the tiny green veins in the leaf dripping off a tree. These details of Divine love from the green vein provides an alleyway for nutritious food to flow from Mother Earth, and allows the sun to stream from Father Sky into the tree in order for it to grow into its most magnificent self. This tender green vein would never question its Divine love for the tree, it just allows this to be done and follows the path of the perfectly created balance of nature.

Deeper Messages of Truth

The ego will try to convince you to attach yourself to substitutes for love because it cannot feel love. It will try to place you in its prison; although, all of this is an illusion. The ego isn't a personal problem, it isn't who you are, it is an illusion. No matter what the situation may be, the ego is never happy. Ego's prayer is always *look without* or look outside yourself and your Spirit's prayer is to *look within* and sing your own exquisite song. Ego chases you around in circles in order to confuse you, it will always try to justify itself, but this can't be achieved. It becomes strengthened by you allowing it to be right and actually you need someone else to be wrong in order to be right. When you do not react to another person's belief in ego concepts, then this effectively dissolves ego. If you react to another person's belief in ego, you may be reacting to a reflection of what is contained inside your own belief system. Loosen the hold of all ego based belief systems now. If you believe that it is part of you then you believe that you were born incomplete, when in fact you were born absolutely complete.

How then do people manifest hurt, distain, hatred and war? It stems from the idea that when you believe something to be real, then it does become real. If you believe you are living in pain and suffering then this is exactly what will be reflected to you because the Universe is believing this is what you want. This reflection or magnetism is called The Law of Attraction. In other words if you say in the morning "This is going to be a bad day" then it will happen or be attracted to you as the Universe is believing this is what you want. It becomes a request or a **send** to the Universe.

If you awake and say, "Thank you for this wonderful and glorious day" then you will have already manifested this glorious wonderful day. Since you have already put out your positive request to the universe and voila, your wonderful and glorious day will arrive. A day to remember! The universe believes you since **you** are the universe. Any thought, anything you do, say or don't do and feel is an affirmation and will be confirmed by the universe. What you put your attention on grows stronger. It is that simple. Perhaps the Law of Attraction was energetically created in order to expose ego?

If you believe there is an ego (<u>E</u>dging <u>G</u>od <u>O</u>ut or <u>E</u>dging <u>G</u>race <u>O</u>ut), then there will be an ego and you will manifest exactly that. In other words, if you worry or fret about life then this is what you attract back to you. So ask yourself, "Why would you want to do that?" Once you truly recognize ego you begin to see, understand and feel everything differently. Your life changes and becomes better because you begin to recognize and dismantle the voice of pain, victimization and emotion of ego. Ego tries to convince you that you are pain not love. Now ask the question, "Does ego actually feel anything?"

The ego will always want to take you away from Spirit since it can not feel Spirit at all. It can not accept White Light and Spirit and in fact moves in a different direction distancing itself completely from love. However, if you are living a life swallowed-up and entrenched by ego then **you** have convinced and allowed yourself to believe that you do not need love and perhaps are not love. Remember that ego resonates on a low, darker and heavier vibration. Once you begin to accept a bit of love from someone or learn to love yourself, this matches your Spirit or sense of love, and this will begin to dismantle the ego, one thought at a time. When the ego is recognized and an awareness of ego is brought to the surface, it then fully dismantles and dissolves. This is the way of moving into grace or Spirit. The

Being or Universe is shifting everybody back to their Original Self and from this Original Self your authentic way of being is created, which is how you live your life on the planet from a point of love. You then realize you have always been love and have believed otherwise.

Do you wish to live from that Original Place or Original Self comprised of love, peace, joy and grace? Or do you want to live from an illusory self? A self containing falsehoods, lies, deceptions, pains and hopelessness, which is all illusion as designed by the energy of ego. This energy is not really an energy but an *idea* in the *mind* which then creates the energy. This energy then manifests itself and becomes a state of pain, suffering and deception. Allow your self to know that the ego no longer exists to the point where you won't have any self-destructing thoughts, ideas, opinions and theories. Just imagine your life free of fear.

To explain further, ego creates the thoughts in the mind as allowed by you, but the mind is connected to the brain. Once you realize that your brain is already filled with White Light and Loving Energy, which is vast, only then will you understand what is being stated here. Actually, the body is illusory since it is in a temporary state, the same as the ego. Now the body or the form is speaking to you and saying, "The veil is thinning and therefore Spirit is coming through more powerfully." Which means old ego concepts are dissolving, leaving you open and surrendered to your Spirit self to shine through you more readily. If the ego thoughts attach themselves to the brain then perhaps you could think of it this way; my brain/my form is an illusion, therefore so is ego an illusion as ego is thought and thought is illusion. So what is real? You are Spirit, Light in human form, meaning your form is a temporary structure for Spirit to move and work through as an open vessel. Your main job on the planet is to know and feel ego is gone and begin to live as Spirit. For Spirit is real!

When you allow ego to dismantle and dissolve it will take with it your old pain-filled stories from childhood, greed, suffering, images of self status and intellectual knowledge. It is within oneself where one finds truth and peace, it is not external of self. The ego embraces all that is not comprised of grace or love since, as stated before, it can't recognize either of these feelings. If ego were to glance in the mirror and see its reflection all that would appear is fear, sadness, dismay and betrayal. You may ask yourself would it recognize or even see itself? Maybe it would become afraid of itself since it is solely based on fear? Or does the ego love its reflection and need to see itself more often? Have you ever looked in the mirror and in your reflection seen traces of fear, sadness, dismay and betrayal? If so you are just looking at the veil or mask of the ego. Tell it to go and it will, as it has no choice but to leave, when recognized.

If you are unaware of your *fear knots* whether this be dismay, or deeply imbedded sadness, or bitterness then the fear knots or ego begins to feed upon itself until you come to a point where the ego reveals itself so much so that you need to see and feel it. This may be in the form of dis-ease. It is therefore very important to let go of fear and *fear not*. When you don't believe the ego's fear knots and you fear not, then you live from grace and grace only. The next question to be asked is: does ego work for grace and just doesn't know it? Or is grace pushing ego up and out in order for the fullest of ego to be exposed? These questions and more will resurface for further exploration throughout this book.

Let's pose the next questions. What would transpire if the illusion of ego was never around and it just wasn't believed? How would this affect our planet earth? Perhaps earth would be one large garden filled with untold beauty, forested with healthy trees and rich soils from the belly of the Mother still in absolute crystal clear shape in its nutrients. The water would be pristine and drinkable and the air breathable no matter where you lived on the planet. So don't you see? When you believe in ego you are truly not loving yourself or the planet, Mother Earth and Father Sky. The pollution on the planet caused by humans was duly created by pain or ego belief. The ego denies you freedom and happiness. It doesn't want anything of a positive nature to surface in your life. It strictly focuses upon pain, war, pollution and tribulations since it can not feel Spirit. So why should you pay attention to it? Why allow yourself to remain in sadness, depression, loneliness and fear? It is just simply no longer necessary to feel these negative emotions during this era of awakening. The world is changing and shifting at a dramatic and most amazing rate. It is a time to re-establish and reposition everything back to love, joy and peace. The beauty and grace of life is emerging and shifting our world. Surrender into this natural exposure, dismantling and dissolving of ego as we remember our grace.

Breathe Into Just Being

Allow yourself the capacity to breathe into *just being* or *just is*, nothing more. Learn to recognize to live as this isness, which is living your life in an absolute stillness and completeness of being. This being is a stillness of grace breathing you, meaning when you are breathing you are being breathed by this stillness. When you are aware of this, then you can *feel* the stillness very quietly and clearly, realize that this feeling has no ego belief systems attached. Notice if your breath is short, shallow or quick, this is usually caused by worry, anxiety, pain, suffering, doubt and uncertainty or symptoms of the ego. Be aware of your breathing and breath. For you are the only one who determines how to use your breath by being consciously aware of your stillness within. You may wish to begin your day in meditation by just paying attention to your breath.

You are already being breathed or lived and it is up to you *how* you breathe. Be gentle. Follow your breathing and be aware of this breath and allow this breath to completely soak into every aspect of who you are; into every cavity within your self. It flows into your organs, muscles, blood, ligaments and all tissues. Breathe into your mind, Spirit, soul, feelings and energy. The flow of Spirit is your breath and a Lightness of who you truly are.

Imagine this – you are a little energy seed which then grows into a bulb with Source within you. Growing you! Breathing you! You are not growing or breathing, you are *being grown and you are being breathed*. Then suddenly, and ever so slowly, the bulb becomes a sprout, then larger it grows until finally a lush, glamorous flower bursts forth from the casing of its green jacket. You have arrived. You are shining in glee, glamorous, excited to show all people and creatures that you are a flower and one of greatness. This greatness is a greatness in trust, faith, knowing and free of ego.

When you recognize ego as illusion and finally free yourself from its heavy weight, you breathe deeply, your life changes and you begin to experience a *Lightness of Being* through this illumination. It's weightless, pure, open, vast and love. Feel this new way or *the new energies*, the next step of the new beginning or new place. Be aware and realize that you are already within the shift of the universe. This is a great time for you to acknowledge that you *are* this amazing shift, yes it is you!

The shift is you!
The shift is already inside of each person.
↓
This enables you to do what *you* want to do.

It is a time for you to move forward within your life, into the beyond and even further into your self of Spirit. Individuals are being placed in people's lives due to the fact that they are collectively helping to guide and move people forward. This real and true movement is extremely important. What is occurring is the beginning of the end of what has been evolving for thousands of years. Eventually you begin to realize and recognize that the shift has already happened. This means you are catching up to the energies which currently exist. You are gently being nudged in its direction and you will transition into what you really wish to do with your life. It is time, and the energies are supporting this shift! Even the sun is shifting but will remain as the sun but differently. It is a time and space; it is a place for all people to recognize they are the same, one and only One, all connected.

It is time to move forward and for everybody to re-unite.
Connect-Oneness
Just Breathe in Life.
It is within the Oneness of self that you extend
outside of yourself, to others and to the
ONE SELF.

There are many pieces of your self that are required to be dismantled. It is within the dismantling process where everything in your life is organized in order to shift further into remembering who you really are. Always be aware of what is occurring within as well as around you.

The way of dismantling involves just loosening the hold and the edginess of all ego-based thoughts. It is a way of allowing yourself to live freely, yet softly and in glory. Place yourself safely, in the purity, non-resistance of life. This is a place of respect which allows for the restructuring of yourself in order to rebuild your memory of who you are. Consider this a safe place and realize that you already exist here and have resided here ever since the beginning your existence.

The concept of existence needs to be clear so that you are able to understand as well as *feel* who you are. Your form of existence means the following: you are water and energy *and* within the water exists your crystals. These crystals are a collective. The inner core of the crystals and the crystal pieces are entangled or inter-woven as a crystal collective. The crystal collective is within and wrapped around each water molecule. Each water molecule forms a part of you. These energetically maintained crystals, within the self, contain the messages of Spirit which originate from the vibration of love. This information or messages have been within the self since the beginning of your time spent as Spirit and then as Spirit in human form.

So, what does this all mean? As you align yourself to your crystals within, you then have access to these crystallized pieces and are able to maintain a greatness in love of just simply being. These crystal pieces are not only maintained within your physical water molecules but energetically as well. While maintaining this relationship with your crystals you arrive at the realization that you are love. You then treat yourself with love and follow your own line of crystals. When you tap into your line of crystals they will guide you throughout your entire life since this is where your Akashic Record exists. These records are the intuitive touches of feelings, activations for messages that relate to moving you forward each and every millisecond of your day. This is the time when all people connect and collect together through the crystals or the Crystal Collectives.

Allow yourself to expand beyond your thoughts and ideas to a place that you believed you could never enter. This place is the place of expansion, ascension and vast. Always remember that you are the Source and the energy that's creating everything. You are the Source that opens up a blossom into a flower, shapes the mountains and births the fawn.

It is now time to recognize that you are
grace-filled, love and passion.
In this new era you will learn to shift, re-shift and reshape
yourself into the best person you can possibly be. You will
immediately recognize that you allowed the belief of ego
to convince you that you were separate from love.
The ability is here within each person to rejuvenate
their way of living and to live this new way of being.
This way of being is an integral part of existing and
realizing yourself as Spirit and nothing more than this.
You will transition from an intellectual mind
to one that embraces the grace of feeling.
Arise to the realization that everything is in
perfect plan and order – everything.

Now you are organized and participating in life at its fullest. Release all that you need to and come forth and forward as who you truly are. Come by your side! Come Be You! The crystals within your true self are activated and speak truth through your breath in **all ways** and **always**. When living from this state of awareness you realize that you are already Light and do not need to become enlightened. Enlightened means to shed Light upon, but now you know you are already this Light.

Reasons, Releasing and Ease

The cement, nails, steel rods in ego are now no longer strong and holding, but rather they are bending and cracking. Everything must bend, break, crack and dismantle if built upon the weak foundation of ego since the materials constructed by ego are now outdated and obsolete. *Now* is the time for the newness of self to be exposed. Everything is being reinvented and we now need to allow our responsibility to take hold of our new way or old way of living. Allow the dismantling and dissolving to take what it needs to take and try to be open and unattached to everything.

Therefore the construction of what was built by ego on our planet is now presently being deconstructed, in much the same way as when an old, mouldy, rotted-out building is bulldozed. What first occurs is the gentle pushing of the structure or ego dismantling, until finally it slowly collapses. It is a time of awarkening, a time of recognition of self, a time of greatness of being, not just simply loving, but being in love with all. It is a magnificent time of re-organizing, re-shifting and transforming. A reconstruction then appears before you. Accept this reconstruction or gentle reshaping of your entire life, which rests upon the foundation of Spirit. You then realize how incredible life can be and really is already.

It is important that you see the ego and its illusion of structure. The structure itself as a belief system can no longer exist. The structure of ego isn't even a structure but a false frame that you were convinced *or* allowed yourself to be convinced that it was solid, sturdy and stable. This flimsy frame is now exposed and being dismantled and dissolved.

As more people awaken, then more dismantling and dissolving of the ego will occur and everything will be made transparent. For example:

1. The dismantling of the *why's* will occur. Individuals seem to have reasons why they do things and they need to understand that these reasons will be irrelevant due to the fact that intellect will no longer matter only your now feelings, not past emotions. Meaning, the intellect is connected to the *emotion* of the old pain-filled story and the intellectual reasons of *why* things happen is also related to the old story. All irrelevant and dismantling.

   When the ego is dismantled or released what remains is ease, intention, a deep knowing, feeling, believing and allowing. A feeling of the present moment, not the emotion connected to a believed past childhood pain-filled story.

2. The dismantling of everything about you, as designed by yourself for believing in ego is happening. Dismantling meaning a transformation, deconstruction of all that does not serve you. No more suffering. Does one need to suffer in the dismantling times? The ego wants emotional suffering and pain but all you need to do is just gently feel these old emotions and then release them. Don't hang onto them and in fact, you will come to a point where you will recognize a transition and you will just shift with the transition and loosen everything.

   Surrender and let go. Become aware of every moment and every thought, feeling and idea - everything. Surrendering is an action that you feel and allow to wash through you.

Soak into this feeling. Surrender the false frame within the structure of ego's illusion. It is time to see the walls or the blockages that you built as you believed the ego's belief system of construction. The energy of surrendering opens up your heart and eyes to see the blockages for what they are – which are illusions. As you surrender the illusions of ego all dissolve and spaces open up for: rejuvenation, a lightened way of being, heart realignment to softness and your body's tissues reconfigure into ease. Your Spirit is then able to shine brightly through these spaces that were once filled with the illusions of blockages. When this happens you awaken with eyes wide open and see all that is around you, maybe for the very first time.

Just allow what is occurring, don't resist and simply believe that all is good, in perfect time and order. Believe that you are **perfect**, **whole** and **complete**.

The old system of ego beliefs, knowing and allowing no longer exists and are being unravelled through the dismantling system. In fact, when you truly allow, know and believe the **new way of being** you recognize and realize that's the only way to live, through your Spirit self. Everything that was created by an ego based way of living is being dismantled and dissolved as included in the Dismantling Table below:

- Dismantling of old belief systems.
- Dismantling of old ideas.
- Dismantling of old allowances.
- Dismantling of old knowings.
- Dismantling of old behaviour patterns.

For complete details of the Dismantling process refer to the Dismantling section of this book.

Dismantling is an energetic movement that places you back to the stillness centre within yourself and to not give into ego thoughts of pain and suffering any power. The contents of this book covers the aspect of moving back into your still self, that is already yourself. It also describes how to shift completely away from ego beliefs. When you ***remember*** or realize that you are Spirit and not ego then other still segments of your life will be seen, displayed or revealed to you. These revelations, "reveal"ations or ***perceived points of existence*** within this time of ***now*** will be revealed to you. Therefore, the revelation of the existence of ego and grace will be thoroughly explored and exposed within the written messages upon each page of this book to ensure that you recognize what does exist and what doesn't exist and to determine what is an illusion and what isn't an illusion.

What exactly does dismantling mean? It means a gentle disallowing or dissolving and a soft way of removing all that needs to be removed in order for the White Light to move through you and others. The White Light is always who you are, but the ego's illusory job is to convince you otherwise. It is a time to reshape yourself and to allow the true self of who you are to reign through you.

Some may say, "I need my ego, it is part of me, for this is the foundation of my existence and my personality." But why would you want to continue to live in pain, with suffering, separation and feeling not enough? Perhaps the only reason would be that you are still believing, knowing and allowing yourself to feel you do not deserve the best. However, the ego will say, "But I do deserve" and your Spirit or grace would then say, "Be love."

To explain this situation: if ego states out loud, "I deserve this and that!" You are actually saying, "I am owed, it's my sense of entitlement because of my old pain-filled story." This is based on fear and low self-worth. Even if you were to state, "I don't deserve this and that!" you are repeating the same thing based upon ego thoughts and feelings of worthlessness. So both of these statements are ego based illusions. Ego based thoughts and your old belief systems which contain many untruths that you have carried around for years since childhood and into adolescence will be dismantled and dissolved.

Shine your ***light of awareness*** through your awakening to the ego, it has no choice but to dissolve. The ego is no longer necessary, and no longer wanted. It is time to shift yourself into this state of awareness.

Ego As An Illusion

The core or the base of The Dismantling process stems from the ego and from the illusion, since it is not real. You were born from White Light and not born from hatred, self worthlessness or not feeling enough. You are the White Light, peace, joy, love and stillness. The programming of the ego illusion began in childhood from your parents/guardian teaching ego based beliefs. Reaching outward from the base of these ego beliefs and thoughts are lifestyles, businesses, personal relationships and all aspects of daily living. During this Age of Dismantling and Transparency everything that has been created by ego based ideas is now being exposed, cleansed and dissolved. Even if your business has been developed from ego's greed then a transition may occur in order to dismantle the ego, thus abling your business to be rebuilt on a stronger foundation.

If you were to explore a Biblical reference, as just one of many references from several religious texts, this particular verse captures this Transparency.

Gospel from Luke 12 (verse 2-4)

"Nothing is covered up that will not be revealed
or hidden that will not be known;
whatever you have said in the dark shall be heard in
the light, and what you have whispered in private
shall be proclaimed upon the housetops."

Another form of dismantling and exposure that will occur is the idea or concept that one needs to become enlightened. Hiking or climbing a mountain, taking a six week course to discover your enlightened self, is an illusion and not required due to the fact that you are ***already*** enlightened. You are already Light, you don't need to enlighten/re-light yourself. You have been convinced that you need to achieve enlightenment. Once you realize and recognize that you are already Light you then begin to feel still and at ease. There is nothing to achieve and nothing to get, it is a very simple, perfect plan. You don't need to read a special book concerning enlightenment as you now know that you are already Light. This is you.

Dismantling is a form of de-structuring or de-stressing your self and a time to fully release old blockages and begin to feel ease. After all, isn't this the purpose of releasing in order to feel ease and a real ease. Allow yourself to be placed in an openness when you read, digest and absorb the dismantling process. It is a time for you to come to realize that you are ok and are capable and able to dismantle everything. Even emotions will be dismantled because when the ego has been dismantled the emotions surrounding the ego also then must leave and dismantle. It is within the dismantling you discover a fullness of freedom, life and love. All three are related and are also the same.

When one dismantles ego thoughts, then you are able to stabilize into just being who you truly are. Therefore, you actually need to leave that part of you that believes in ego and how everything is all about you and who you are, what you achieve, the amount of money you have or don't have, the number of degrees you have obtained or haven't obtained, the need to be right, the need to have more and the need to show others that "you know a lot." These are all ego thoughts and the most peculiar thing about the ego belief system is that some people fully believe it, honour it and want more of it. They may not even recognize the eventual pain that accompanies the ego. In fact, the ego feeds off the pain, it loves pain and will create more pain or negativity – it is gluttonous!

If one is able to acquire the realization that ego is illusion, then it is never spoken about again. You simply don't need to even say "ego is illusion" because it is no longer a part of your thinking or belief system. Just by saying that it is an illusion gives it its illusory power back to ego and ignites ego manifestation. Why would you wish to do this?

Pay attention, be aware and notice as the dismantlings occur everything is still being held together. There is an energetic ***hold*** or holding space pattern that is present through Source/Archangels/Guides/The Being. Since you are being warmly and tenderly held, why not enter and step into a life that is free of the illusion and ego. Take a ***slide step***, not side step, for an easy, smooth and rhythmic transition. Much like when you accept the love of somebody giving you a slurp of their smoothie milkshake – accept this gift and allow this love to gulp into your whole self.

Observe the illustration of *Ego Dismantling* (Figure 2) as depicted within a swirl or vortex held tightly, yet tenderly by the White Light. The spin or energy swirl is the dismantling of all ego based beliefs. The point at the base of the swirl is your authentic, solid point of existence and true love. It is also the Oneness, All Truths, Freedom, No Polarities and so much more.

Ego Dismantling

(Figure 2)

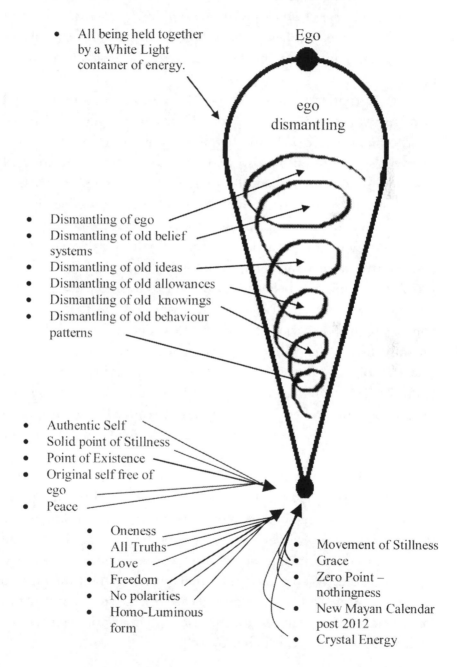

- All being held together by a White Light container of energy.

Ego

ego dismantling

- Dismantling of ego
- Dismantling of old belief systems
- Dismantling of old ideas
- Dismantling of old allowances
- Dismantling of old knowings
- Dismantling of old behaviour patterns

- Authentic Self
- Solid point of Stillness
- Point of Existence
- Original self free of ego
- Peace

  - Oneness
  - All Truths
  - Love
  - Freedom
  - No polarities
  - Homo-Luminous form

  - Movement of Stillness
  - Grace
  - Zero Point – nothingness
  - New Mayan Calendar post 2012
  - Crystal Energy

Ego has been allowed and accepted by us in all areas of our *life selves*, which includes the body, mind, Spirit, emotion and energy. But now it is recognized as illusion since war, injury, abuse and torture *can no longer occur on this planet anymore*. These situations and others have been manifested by people focusing and believing in ego beliefs of pain, deserving, revenge, a sense of entitlement and of hatred.

Yet all that is manifested has *All Ready* been manifested prior to your arrival on this planet. If what you say is all ready manifested as grace, love and involving your soul's purpose then does ego's manifestation also appear to be pre-planned and all ready manifested by you and for you? This sounds a bit confusing so let's simplify and determine how all of this works. Firstly, are you a believer in karma and that it needs to be cleared in order for your dharma or soul's purpose to come forth? This is all illusion and requires a dismantling and dissolving in and of itself. There was a time when the belief in karma was true and alive and still may be believed to be true and alive today. What this means is you are required to clear all karma in order to live a full, soul purpose filled life. If ego is illusion, therefore so is karma as there is nothing to clear. This becomes more evident when you begin to live from a vastness or openness of grace, love, peace, joy and passion. When you are living self-realized, self-actualized and self-aligned to Spirit, then you can not be living as pain or suffering.

That being said, would the next question then be, "Will karma completely disappear *as* ego dismantles?" Yes, of course it will disappear as there will be no ego or karma to clear and the dismantling of the structure of the ego will be completed. You begin to realize that all components of ego are illusion and the excavation of the manifested ego reveals the false pretense of its make-believe structure with no solid foundation. As you allow the old ego structure to deconstruct its form, beneath it is an ancient sacred place still in its original position, foundation and stance, which is Spirit.

Therefore what is being said is that everything is All Ready available for you to receive and accept. ***Everything*** and ***all things*** were all ready custom ordered by you and for you before you squeezed into your physical human form. How wonderful! So what you want then truly wants you, fully in this "Now" moment. Know and feel you have the end result already, without any attachments. To start at the end is only the beginning. Meaning you just know you have already acquired that funky art studio you have dreamed about for weeks or even years. You feel it, smell it, touch it in your visual self and simply allow the universe to shift the energies to gift it to you. Another example, perhaps someone is seeking an engineering job in Europe and they know, believe and feel it is there already manifested for him/her. Therefore they no longer need to seek. Do you see dear reader how each of you has manifested everything? All you need to do is relax, believe, loosen ego beliefs, fully accept with ***arms wide open*** all ready for the embrace of what you have manifested already?

Arise to the fact that we are all living from a place of peace.
A place of absolute joy, where you are embracing who
you truly are and nothing more or less than this.
Stop believing who you are not!

As it is being revealed, the ego may attempt to create some form of chaos and distain just before it becomes dismantled and dissolved. Within the revelation or the revealing of the ego it gets annoyed and will attempt further to confuse you but it is only having a temper tantrum. Once you realize that you are grace and filled with love, joy and peace then you begin to shift within yourself to a new way of being. Which means you shift into being the original you. You often hear the phrase, "Just be yourself," and what exactly does this mean? When you live from a state of grace you begin to just know that you are free already and there is nothing other than this freedom.

When you shift and become a person of positive ideas, behaviours, thoughts, feelings, then you will feel real freedom. This shift or change is the transformed state of consciousness and it is extremely important you begin to set ego beliefs free. The ego is being exposed by you. It has been able to hide in your unawakened state for many years or possibly life times. When you are not in an awakened state you are living from the trance of the ego which means you are unaware of every single now moment. You become numb and unaware of a beautiful way of living. You may be unaware of what is going on, which is exactly what the ego wants:

1. For you to be unawakened to the fact that you are grace. Ego wants you to forget and move away from Spirit and back into painful situations.

2. For you to not know you are worthy and filled with love, joy and peace.

3. For you to live outside of this now present moment and to continue to worry.

4. For you to not recognize that you may serve as a vessel for Spirit to move through you.

Reverse these above ego programmed falsehoods and state:

1. "I am grace."

2. "I am love, joy and peace."

3. "I am now living in the now."

4. "I am a vessel for the Spirit to move through me. I am experiencing the feeling of knowing I am a vessel or an *Instrument of Peace*." This is gloriously remembered in the lyrics to a song entitled, *Instrument of Peace* as inspired by the poetic words of St. Francis of Assisi and sung by Amy Sky and Marc Jordan, see below. Remember this is who you are, an Instrument for Spirit to move through you.

Instrument of Peace

"Where there is hatred, let me bring love ...
Where there is silence, let me sing praise ...
For when we give we will receive ...
Make me an Instrument of Peace ..."

(Moccio, Stephan. *Instrument of Peace*, performed
by Amy Sky and Marc Jordan. Latte Music/Sony
Music Publishing/Sing Little Penguins. 2006.)

As one enters into an awakened state of being or the vortex of existing within the space of the now, you then recognize that everything has been in perfect plan and order. You are just simply here to be love and to serve. The history of the ego's existence has been allowed in order for the energy of love to pull all people through and to watch how the ego dismantles and dissolves. Therefore it is a time for all people to experience the true way of being.

All will dismantle in order to remember their existence as grace. The purpose of ego has been now fulfilled and it is time to release all that needs to be released. How is this related to an individual choosing a path of darkness by following the ego? Release the ego stories and assist others in releasing their ego story. The sooner you awaken and release the ego, along with releasing painful stories you've been holding onto, then the sooner you may assist others on their path to dismantling the ego. What this means is the following: when you choose to live and follow the way of grace, you then engage in the path of inspiration or being in-Spirit. A sense of clarity presents itself as you push through ego and the collective ego based way of being. You begin to feel a comfort of all that is real, which is grace, love, joy, peace and passion. It is a solidity of stillness or a who you truly are and a recognition of a deeper self.

It is a time to continue to push your self through the ego based way of being. Actually, as you are manoeuvring through some of ego's manifested thickness you realize it is just an illusion anyway and it's not thick! In fact the ego is now holding up the White Flag and surrendering. Remember that when the White Light shines into the darkness, the darkness disappears. The ego fizzles out.

The closer you get to the end of your belief in the ego, the more dysfunctional the ego belief becomes. The dysfunction is the low point of feeling depression, loss and emptiness. The following diagram *The Beginning and End of Believing Ego* (Figure 3) illustrates the continuum of the ego and the steps of the evolution of an individual shifting back to their Original Self. As illustrated, the ego dismantling steps begin with birth and evolve along the path of believing the ego teachings to finally realizing the ego is only an illusion, then shifting or remembering your Original, peace-filled self. When you begin to remember who you are, the door opening to ego belief systems then closes behind you, never to be opened again. Notice how in between each section in the Figure 3 diagram structure there is a small ***slide ribbon arrow*** which demonstrates the ease of the movement from one section to the next section.

*Realize that all components of ego are illusion
and the excavation of the manifested ego
reveals the false pretense of its make-believe
structure with no solid foundation.*

The Beginning and End of Believing Ego
(Figure 3)

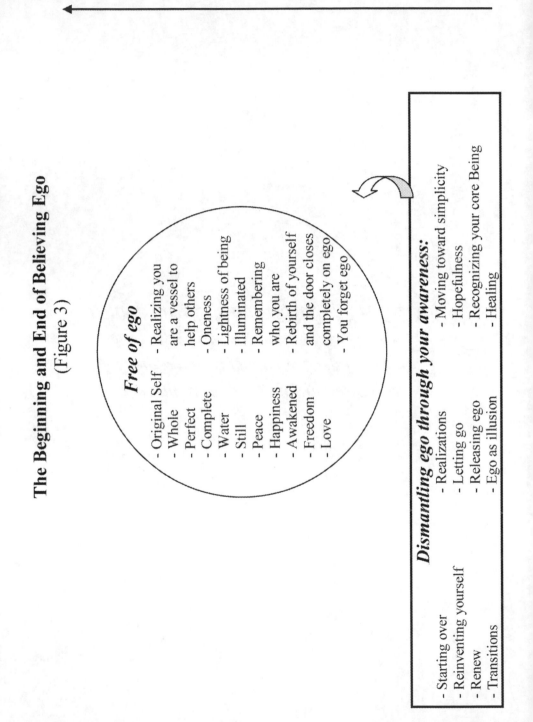

Free of ego

- Original Self
- Whole
- Perfect
- Complete
- Water
- Still
- Peace
- Happiness
- Awakened
- Freedom
- Love

- Realizing you are a vessel to help others
- Oneness
- Lightness of being
- Illuminated
- Remembering who you are
- Rebirth of yourself and the door closes completely on ego
- You forget ego

Dismantling ego through your awareness:

- Starting over
- Reinventing yourself
- Renew
- Transitions

- Realizations
- Letting go
- Releasing ego
- Ego as illusion

- Moving toward simplicity
- Hopefulness
- Recognizing your core Being
- Healing

Ascension

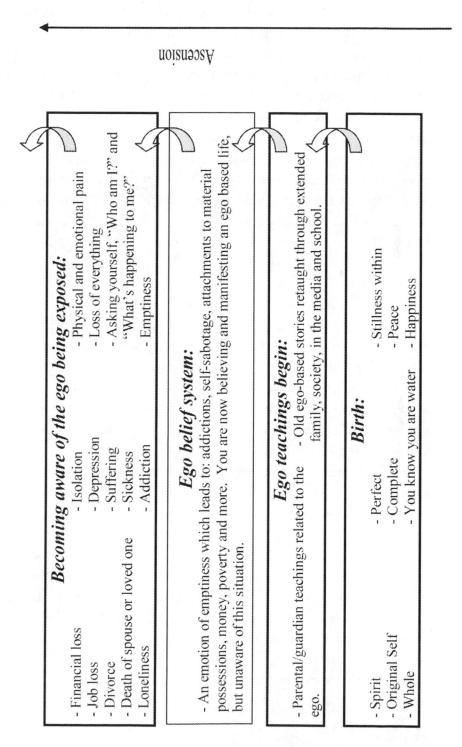

Becoming aware of the ego being exposed:

- Financial loss
- Job loss
- Divorce
- Death of spouse or loved one
- Loneliness

- Isolation
- Depression
- Suffering
- Sickness
- Addiction

- Physical and emotional pain
- Loss of everything
- Asking yourself, "Who am I?" and "What's happening to me?"
- Emptiness

Ego belief system:

- An emotion of emptiness which leads to: addictions, self-sabotage, attachments to material possessions, money, poverty and more. You are now believing and manifesting an ego based life, but unaware of this situation.

Ego teachings begin:

- Parental/guardian teachings related to the ego.
- Old ego-based stories retaught through extended family, society, in the media and school.

Birth:

- Spirit
- Original Self
- Whole

- Perfect
- Complete
- You know you are water

- Stillness within
- Peace
- Happiness

The teachings of ego belief systems begin with family, society, school and through the media. Yet all are born perfect, whole and complete in love, peace and stillness. When one begins to believe ego teachings and then builds upon this belief structure this adds to their own falsehood perceptions of not being worthy, self-sabotaging and not good enough. As this belief continues to build, an emptiness develops and possible addiction, disease and loss. This may be considered a low point of existence where one then experiences the exposure of ego and begins to question why? They may wonder, "There must be more to life?" "Why am I so sad?" "What is going on with me?" As one continues to ask questions then the dismantling begins and clarity starts to shine its light upon the dark places that you have believed for many years.

You now begin to let go, release, start again but differently this time. You transition and evolve into releasing the hold of everything and eventually you awaken to who you truly are. *Then* realizations and recognitions happen for you. A freeing takes place, the weight releases and you realize that you are just love and always have been and just believed otherwise or in an illusion. *The illusion ends here and now, allow truth to dissolve it.* Allow truth to loosen all ties entangled or knotted by the lies created by ego's illusions. Just say to yourself, "The sojourn ends here in this now moment. The illusions I have been believing, allowing and living now stops in this present now moment. My real sojourn does not include ego illusions. I surrender, let go and forget all ego illusions. I give thanks and praise and live a life that is rich and full in grace."

Even the Law of Attraction at some point in time will become a Law of Attraction only for the higher vibrational ideas and thoughts. Meaning ego will no longer be recognized through the Law of Attraction. It will only place the attraction back to the positive, high vibrations rather than the negative toxic pieces of pain, suffering and hatred. Therefore, who you truly are, which is Source will be reflected back to the Source or matched to you, as Source. Ego was at one time adhered to, listened to and believed, but *now* is starting to not be energetically heard. In fact, literally you will not be able to hear ego or feel its vibration at all due to the high vibration of the planet and your own radiating vibration of heart love. As one person awakens to who they are this increases the vibration of the planet through the high vibration of heart. As more people loosen the belief of ego and live from their heart this will inevitably assist the entire planet.

You as the reader need to feel and understand how you can help somebody who continues to believe and live through their old ego stories. Just by you awakening to the love of yourself and loosening ego will greatly assist. This heart energetic vibration will nudge the energies within this person and allow them to slightly reshape their thoughts and to expand into the feelings of love. Our core self does not want to hurt anybody or anything.

When you remember who you truly are your senses sharpen and become clearer. This purity of love of self heightens and you feel and see all or everything:

<u>Every day I see</u>

- Beauty
- Sunshine
- Clarity
- Softness
- Round soft parts in life
- Simplicity

<u>I feel</u>
- Love deeply
- Passion completely
- The stillness of peace

<u>I hear</u>
- Crisps of leaves
- A grasshopper skipping on the belly of the Mother Earth

I taste
- One crunchy sweet carrot
- Water sprinkled with zesty lemon
- Fresh, moist air

I touch
- Everything and now it's so clear to me, and it's so refreshing

I smell
- The floral inner essence of a fragrant rose

I experience **all** things from and only from love. This is where one needs to live and exist; it is a place of greatness, simplicity and a knowing. It is wrapped in a warmth, calmness, sweetness and Light.

The way in which you participate in life is determined by love and by nothing else. The ego is not love, caring and joy, but fear, anxiety, worry, and anger. It is now a time for people to recognize the ego and ask deeper questions:

1. What are my thoughts saying to me?

2. Is ego a separate voice or my own voice? In other words, is it a parental voice I am hearing and feeling or is it society, the media and/or a school teacher's voice?

3. Does the voice of ego say harmful thoughts?

4. Does the ego resonate within a certain place in my body?

5. Is the ego trying to convince me that I am not grace?

6. Does the ego try to convince me that I am separate and/ or better than others? For example, thoughts of: "I am smarter than, wealthier than, skinnier than," and so on. The ego will also try to convince you that you are not worthy: "I am not smart, I am poor, I am unworthy."

These extremes are ego based and illusions. All people are the same and nobody is different from one another since all are One. All are connected and the ego is attempting to make you believe that you are not one, but separate. There is no intellectual definition of the self. Yes, perhaps you indicate that you have brown hair and green eyes, others will say they, themselves, have dark skin and black hair, male/female, therefore making you the unique self. This is the self defined by your authentic self and perhaps the term authentic should be changed due to the fact that all people are love and express love uniquely. Remember that your Spirit, your Essence is the same as the person beside you, in front of you, behind you, living in the mansion or homeless on the street. We are all the same, we are One. The piece of you that lives forever is your eternal Spirit, the physical form disappears and dissolves. Only the Spirit remains forever and shifts back to the larger Being or the White Light. It is present in this explanation where one finds a resolution or a revelation of what is going on inside of oneself.

7. Ego belief systems will try to convince you that you need to destroy all grace pieces within you, but remember nothing will ever destroy your Spirit, ever! You do have a choice or maybe there is *no longer a choice*. The only choice is grace and love, not ego. Why would you choose ego and pain? So there really is no choice.

Furthermore, there is free will but this does not mean *choice*, it poses the question: do you *will to be free*? Allow your will, which is who you are already, this means willingness to feel love, peace and your strength or power of being Spirit. Free will means you are free and it is wrapped tightly and between the energetic vibration of freedom which is defined as:

- you are willing to serve others and the planet
- you are willing to just be
- you are willing to let go
- you are willing to be free
- you are willing to be love

Begin to realize that you are already free, love, serving and have surrendered into your willingness to live as peace.

A Note

When reading this particular book you will begin to free yourself and recognize you are already love, perfect, whole and complete. There's a common thread that is woven throughout the entire book which includes several phrases of repetitions that are specifically placed to emphasize certain concepts and feelings. As you shift and move forward you begin to unravel, then reshape and reshift your way of existence. When you arrive in a place of contentment and joy you then are able to receive and allow yourself to live in a place of absolutes. *Absolutes* of love, joy and peace and you *absolutely* know you are this!

Just simply live freely and lovingly from the place where you are able to reset yourself as refresh or undo buttons. When you reset yourself, as if a button on the computer were being used, you then move, reset or rewire your entire being and begin to realize you were perfect already. When you shift, the energies shift and change around you in a tremendous and beautiful fashion. You then begin to see, feel, taste, and touch life very differently. When you are ego free, you are free and grace fully moves through you and touches others, as well.

You savour the sweetness of life in your new way of existing. This is a wonderful way of receiving and the giving of love. Believe that you and all people on the planet are the crystals of energy and the messages are interwoven within these crystals. These crystals are also contained in your cellular, molecular, energetic, spiritual imprints. It is all here within this place of realism where truth is occurring; truth meaning crystal clear energy of love – this is who you are!

This is a time for the re-formation of life. A time when the re-forming of the unfoldment of self is occurring. It is time for you to begin to realize that a new way of living, a new way of beginning is happening now and will continue to evolve until the fullness or completion of the evolution takes place. Liken to a caterpillar that needs to cocoon and transition by holding itself close in order for the metamorphosis process to release it into the butterfly. You too will be living like a butterfly, since you have shifted or transitioned to knowing that ego is illusion and you no longer need to remember the cocoon. When aware of the ego teachings and you release these teachings or belief system, at that point you do not remember the ego. You are just born or birthed into remembering who you truly are as you unfurl your wings. Within the unfolding of the butterfly's wings is the instinctual remembrance that it was born to fly. When you trust, you follow the natural instinct that you were created from and born with.

The tiny coloured scales or feathers on the monarch butterfly wings are not only the symbol of beauty, but one of peace"full"ness. The feathers or scales within each wing represent many colours, when combined, create an amazing sparkle and shimmering glare or reflection. Every tiny feather has been placed very carefully on each wing as a piece of Source/White Light created only for that specific butterfly. The feather has its own duty and job. One job is to radiate its vibrant shades of orange, gold, red and yellow and to say, "Look at me for I am who I am. I am a bright shiny, gentle, feather connected to the whole wing. I am extremely important for the wing. I am the wing, for without me there would be existing an empty hole. I am part of the team of feathers created in a perfect design for all to see. I am peace, love, joy, passion and compassion."

Even this tiny feather or scale knows its job to radiate Source/White Light through its glorious colours. It also knows, believes and allows itself to feel honoured, blessed, free, peaceful and joy-filled. The feather works as a team member with the other glimmering sequined feathers to create an integral and unique wing design. These specific designs on the monarch butterfly wings are not only beautiful and glamorous but also provides protection from predators. In perfect plan, all creatures have some type of protection barrier. Without these protective feathers or scales on their wings the death of the butterfly would be imminent.

As humans, you too, are the tiny feathers placed on earth to work hand-in-hand with all of nature as one influences the other. You, as a human influence other humans by your actions, language, feelings and energy. If you are filled with passion, bliss and joy, you exist as that tiny butterfly scale does – in Source – in Love – in Peace. You are consciously aware of your surroundings and you feel and understand the necessity to join and become One with nature. All is created in order to bring forward peace, love, trust, and joy.

The brightly coloured monarch butterfly wings are able to capture the sun's reflection and reflect it back to others. You too are able to capture and reflect back the sun's rays generated from Source/White Light. Do not be afraid of **Shining Brightly**, even if you feel that you are the only one doing so, just remember that one tiny feather on the butterfly wing will bring some passion to the wing and an energy attraction for other feathers to come and join the wing of feathers.

As you begin to take notice of how you flow in life, you then become consciously aware of everything you say, feel, do and even think. Simply be aware of "you". Are you the glimmering sequined gold, red or orange scale on the butterfly wings or are you feeling empty of shine and lustre? Have you decided to not unfold your wings and therefore refusing to remember who you are; a butterfly of freedom.

Every human has a purpose and reason for living on this planet, which is to love. You are God/Source/White Light, so let this shine through you and flow with life, be peace-filled, joy-filled, kind and loving. Fly as the butterfly's wings and feel the wind on your cheeks, taste the air's moisture and touch the sun's warmth. Allow the butterfly to fly through this book and carry you upon its wings of metamorphosis or the unfoldment to remembering that you are Spirit.

Part II

Dismantling

When you begin to follow your intuitive self, this will lead you to what is already manifested for you.

Introduction

*The collective goal NOW upon the planet
is to expose the ego as illusion.*

This section will focus specifically on what is being dismantled and how to ease your life as you move through the process of dismantling or transitioning. This transition or metamorphosis is shifting you into a life of ease and contentment rather than one filled with worry, anxiety, sadness, depression, fear and anger. This slide towards freedom, which is already inside of you is *all ready*, and just waiting for your awareness; for you to recognize its grace of freedom.

Exactly what is being dismantled and how you can unfold this process will be discussed and as stated previously everything constructed by ego will be revealed or exposed, then dismantled and dissolved. Meaning, the dismantling of the ego then dissolves into its own illusion and disappears. The collective goal now upon the planet is to expose the ego as illusion. As we allow ego belief systems to become more illusionary, they dismantle and we realize that a new, stronger structure is already formed in place. It is the new structure for living. The best part is the fact that this new structure already exists and is waiting for you to just be aware of it. It is called *the structure of love* which, for some, has been veiled by the ego's structure which is thin, wobbly and is no longer holding together. Ego's structure is similar to a flimsy building held with nails that have rusted and broken; the walls falling apart due to defective material that was used in its construction and finally its cement is no longer supporting the foundation because this cement was not really cement, but fluffy dust. The structure of love wants your recognition or your remembering, then you will see and even feel it to be true.

The ego then, is in-material and when exposed it is recognized that a whole new structure needs to be built in order for sustainability. It's essential to recognize we are that *already* and we *all ready* have the new structure in place which is love, grace, peace and joy.

In this part of the book are two sections on dismantling. Read each one gently and carefully, feel the messages and absorb their teachings. The first section entitled "*The Dismantling Curriculums*" will introduce you to the *Ego Curriculum*, *The "R" Points of Existence*, and *Ego Curriculum Questions*. The second is the *Now Curriculum and Questions.* Interwoven within these two based curriculums are the specific dismantlings of old ego based thoughts, ideas, philosophies and behaviours. All explained and discussed in detail as gifted to you!

Be open.

The Dismantling Curriculums

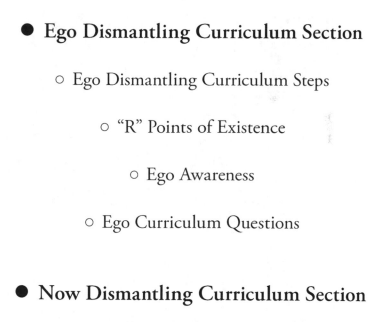

- **Ego Dismantling Curriculum Section**

  - Ego Dismantling Curriculum Steps

  - "R" Points of Existence

  - Ego Awareness

  - Ego Curriculum Questions

- **Now Dismantling Curriculum Section**

  - Now Curriculum

  - Now Curriculum Questions

*As we allow the ego to become more illusionary
it dismantles and we realize that a new structure
is already formed in place that is stronger.*

The Ego Dismantling Curriculum Section

- Ego Dismantling Curriculum Steps

- "R" Points of Existence

- Ego Awareness

- Ego Curriculum Questions

The Ego Dismantling Curriculum

T he ego will be recognized and exposed by the following processes of the *ego dismantling curriculum*, which will move you through the different steps of awareness. As you gently read each step, absorb and feel what is being suggested. Allow yourself to assimilate the truths and to be open and willing to release ego thoughts of pain, fear and suffering.

Begin with a tenderness for your inner self.

Ego Dismantling Curriculum Steps:

1. The first step involves the *intellect* and how it associates itself with ego. The intellect needs to understand and have knowledge concerning what the ego is and the structure of its identity, which is suffering and pain. The ego passes itself off as instinct and intelligence. It's the inner dialogue that draws you in to assume that you are the source of self-created intelligence. This step also involves intellectually understanding how you have identified yourself according to your thoughts, which is ego. Ego's job is to convince you that you are a separate individual, a victim of loneliness, fear-filled, revengeful and angry. It does not recognize the feeling of love and grace.

2. The second step requires you to just simply be **aware** of ego thoughts in your mind. These thoughts are always judgemental, so be aware of "I am not enough, "I am too tall, too short," "I am not worthy," "I am too shy," "I am not loveable," "I am better," "I am more authentic than others," and "Look at me," plus various other statements.

3. Third step involves **emotions**. Observe how you feel when you hear "an ego chatter" slip into your thoughts? If you feel negative and/or judgemental then this is exactly what ego wants you to feel physically. This may result in feeling heavy, tired, cold, achy, unfocused, foggy thinking, hungry or without an appetite, or other emotions or symptoms. The key is to be aware of these emotions or symptoms in order to release them. As your awareness expands and strengthens you will break free from one ego thought at a time or several, it is up to you. Feel your journey of releasing or dismantling more fully. Release, dismantle ... be free and actually recognize you already are free. In the past you have allowed ego belief systems to dominate and convince you that you are not free.

4. The fourth step engages you to feel better about yourself and realize that the ego is self-created and simply not real. You were already born perfect, whole and complete. You are not born as suffering or pain. You were born as love and grace and it **is** as simple as this since you are Spirit.

5. The fifth step requires you to realign your thinking and realize that ego can not live in the now moment.

These five steps of recognizing and releasing ego and shifting into the now moment, being aware of the moment **and** being aware of ego based thoughts become easier as your awareness increases and heightens. When you are aware of these thoughts they dismantle. If you are not aware of the ego-based thoughts then you will continue to allow them to dominate your life. Engage your self in being conscious of one singular thought that speaks of ego and you will be able to recognize and dismantle other thoughts. **Then** you begin to realize that you are no longer identified with the ego teachings or beliefs of pain and fear. ***You are just love, peace and joy.***

Be aware of what is transpiring with your thoughts then begin to say to these thoughts "***Be gone and leave.***" Ego thoughts no longer serve any purpose in your life. Practice moving into the now moment and discover that you are surrounded by beauty and only beauty in that moment. If you live outside of the moment and worry about the past or the future then you are not feeling, tasting, touching, smelling and hearing the all ready perfection in this now space or moment. When residing in this moment you are truly in a space that is empty of thought. Be open and allow all things to assist you to move through this moment and continue on to the next moment. If you are resting quietly on a white sandy beach and you are living presently in the moment you will see the wobbly little crab toddling right beside you as it dashes over the sand dunes towards the ocean's waves. You may sense the heat of the sun warming every cell of your body as you are enjoying the taste of a mango while its juice drips sweetly from its ripened fruit.

When you live in the now everything is gifted to you and you are able to see, feel, taste, touch and hear all that is around you. If you are not living in the now then you will miss much about life. You will miss the angel signs gently urging you to walk this way, sit here, call this friend, read this book, pick up this shimmery feather or stone. Allow each moment to carry your attention to intention to the next moment of seeing, feeling, smelling, tasting and touching glory all around you, no matter what circumstance.

Furthermore, be fully aware of where your body is right now. Are you standing, sitting or lying down? Wherever you are, experience everything, including the chair, couch, the floor and listen carefully to what is going on around you. If you are eating something then taste if completely, for in fact eating is a great now moment exercise. Feel and be aware of everything around you, in front of you, behind you and touching you.

Now ask yourself these questions: "Am I feeling distressed in this now moment?" "Am I feeling anger, anxiety or fear?" The answer can only be no, because there is nothing to fear or be stressed about right now. Even if you were to believe that there is something to be stressed about, then just observe it and see it for what it is; an illusion of the past or future. Is it real? Or is it a figment of your imagination that just wants to be real? A figment will become real even if you imagine it since this figment wants the energy to manifest. A figment may be a singular existence. When you imagine this figment to be true, then it is true and manifests itself to be real. So what does this mean? If you are living in a very pin-pointed now moment and you are aware of everything, but suddenly you begin to feel anxiety or fear, for example about a job interview scheduled for tomorrow, then what? Observe this feeling as you live from this now moment and allow it to reveal itself to you. Is it real? The interview hasn't happened yet so how could this fear and anxiety be real in this now moment? Realize that it just can't be real.

The ego wants you out of the now moment and living in the past or future. You only leave the moment when you pay attention to the thoughts that may be ego influenced, so allow them to move away. Tell them to "Be gone." Don't hang onto them; just continue to do what you are doing. There is a form of mindful meditation that allows those thoughts to move through you. There will come a point when you will not require a mindful meditation as you will no longer have any ego mind-filled thoughts to move through you.

As you travel along in the now moments, one moment melts into the next and eventually the ego is gone and you are living only from grace and grace alone. You begin to realize and know that your beingness is already here and everything is all ready for you. This has been messaged to you several times in this book. The Universe, The Being, Source, White Light, it really doesn't matter what term you use, is just awaiting your *arrival* from the *departure* of ego-based thoughts to a sort of "Wonderful Land of All Readiness." Do you understand what is being said here? This is the collective consciousness, The Shift and The New Way of Being or the term ***The New Earth*** as stated by Eckhart Tolle in his book with the same title, *A New Earth* (Tolle, Eckhart. *A New Earth*. Toronto, Canada. Penguin Publishing. 2005.) is already here. People are just catching up to this phenomena of releasing ego and stepping into the known that is all ready for you, not the unknown, which is ego trying to convince you that all is unknown.

If you are not aware of ego then you believe it intellectually to be true and allow yourself to continue to believe in it and therefore manifest more. If you know ego you would be aware of it and loosen your allowance of its teachings of falsehoods. When you are aware of allowing ego, you know and observe ego thoughts, then you remain silent and begin to release ego beliefs.

All is being dismantled in order for you to return to your Original Self. If you are being shifted back to the original self then all is known. Original means known or knowing which indicates that you just know everything is great and ok in this now moment and all now moments. Eventually you will recognize that the now moment does not exist because you are living fully present as an already enlightened being. Then the now disappears and you feel the ***all***, the Oneness. You no longer need to be so focused upon the now moment since you are now living from Essence. You shine, glisten and ask, "How may I serve?" This freeing of the ego drips away all thoughts of destruction. You then fill or gain in grace into these empty spaces that were once filled with believing in the ego's illusion.

"R" Points of Existence

The Ego Dismantling Curriculum steps are extended into the following *"R" Points of Existence*. These Points of Existence summarize the shifting of ego to the points of living your true self of love.

1. Point of Recognition

The point of recognition is the point in your life when you recognize that you are Spirit first and your physical form is secondary. Spirit is grace, love and peace, and this is who you truly are, nothing more. ***Know*** you are Spirit and ***feel*** this to be true. This allows you to recognize ego beliefs. Yes, you are in the human form which is the vessel, tool or instrument for Spirit to move and work through you. Read the following passage of words ***peaced*** together in St. Francis of Assisi's poem intimating for you to live as an instrument of peace to serve. Thus living according to who you truly are.

St. Francis of Assisi Prayer

Lord, make me an instrument of your peace.
Where there is hatred, let us sow love;
Where there is injury, pardon;
Where there is doubt, faith;
Where there is despair, hope;
Where there is darkness, light;

And where there is sadness, joy.
O Divine Master, grant that I may not so
much seek to be consoled as to console;
to be understood, as to understand;
to be love, as to love.
For it is in giving that we receive;
it is in pardoning that we are pardoned;
and it is in dying that we are born to eternal life.
Amen
St. Francis of Assisi (1181-1226)

2. Point of "Reveal"ation

This is the point of revealing ego and catching ego thoughts of pain, fear and suffering. It is the true awareness of hearing ego thoughts say, "I am not good enough," "Nobody will like me" or "I am better than others." Once you are able to catch these ego thoughts you are then able to dissolve them. Eventually they will automatically dissolve because you know they are not real, thus the point of "reveal"ation or revelation.

3. Point of Realization

At this point in life, you realize that you are ***already enlightened***. You are already light, love, happiness, joy and peace. You don't need to read any books or attend a conference or workshop, hike the highest mountain or live in an ashram to discover enlightenment and happiness, as you are already this! This point of realization is a realization that everything is already ***all ready*** there for you. You just need to accept!

4. Point of Reconciliation

During this point you deeply reconnect and remember that you are Spirit. You become fully aware of Spirit as who you truly and really are. You may even say, thank you to ego for its lessons of knowing what is real and what is illusion. This simply means you are reconciling ***all*** or coming back to your Original Self = Spirit.

5. *Point of Realignment*

The final point is a now point in life where you realign everything and be the living true Authentic Self of Essence. You are the movement of stillness, you are the truest of Spirit, you are love, you are also:

- the sunset and sunrise
- the synchronized being
- the lullaby of music
- peace
- Oneness of All Beings
- vast and open
- happiness and joy
- ascended
- simplicity or just being
- guided action from heart
- the open vessel or instrument

As you naturally move through these "R" Points of Existence allow yourself to just feel your self at each point. Each "R" point may happen during different periods of your life or all points may occur spontaneously for you. It is nothing more than **Knowing**, **Allowing** and **Believing** who you truly are. I have channeled a deck of eighty cards called *The Know, Allow and Believe Cards* (Published by The Waterview Space. Ontario, Canada. 2012.) where you choose a card daily, from the collection. These cards are channeled from **Abraham**, a large White Light Collective Soul and Great Teachers upon the planet. It was an honour to channel these cards. Each card speaks about how to Know, Allow and Believe who you truly are. The allowing is first, once you allow yourself to be open then the believing and knowing of self emerges. In other words, the emergence of self occurs through the 5 points of recognition, re"veal"ation, realization, reconciliation and realignment.

Ego Awareness

In order for you to become aware of ego-based thoughts it is important to understand that you must constantly monitor your thoughts that you allow to inform your thinking. If you allow fear-based or judgemental thoughts, then negative emotions will attach to these thoughts and create unwanted scenarios. How can you become aware and capture ego thoughts *just prior* to them forming and negate their impact on your life?

If an ego-based thought arrives that states: "I am not good enough," how can you anticipate this suggestion even before it arrives? As you begin to recognize or be aware of ego you will begin to notice what scenarios, events, situations and conversations trigger the ego thoughts. Perhaps you experience more ego thoughts when at work, in social situations, on certain celebrated holidays with specific people. You may wonder about the time just prior to any ego thought that arrives, as it's a very tiny millisecond or gap between thoughts. How do I just stay in ease? Is there a special code or key to use which keeps the ego completely free from you so that you remain in an awareness of knowing ego is an illusion? The truth is the key, that you are Spirit, you know this is true and live from there, from this place of peace.

As more people become aware of the illusion of ego and the truth that you already are enlightened. Then, this higher vibration of self influences others which in turn influences the planet. This higher vibration will allow people to slide into the realized or *All Readiness* state more quickly. For those of you who are still questioning what can stop the ego so that I no longer need to even be aware of it, here is a simple exercise: move into a quiet space in your mind, listen and feel in the now moment. Focus and keep your attention upon what you see, feel, smell, taste and hear in this moment. If you become aware of an ego thought, then pay attention to the pin-pointed tiny gap that happened just before the ego thought arrived. Can you find and feel that gap? What is that gap? Become aware of this millisecond gap and if an ego thought arrives or illusion arrives ask what its purpose is. Does it have a job? However, really its only job is to create more questions, confusion and suffering to keep you allowing your negative story or judgements to remain intact.

Is it possible that the energies now present on the planet are able to penetrate more deeply into assisting us in presenting a secret key, aimed at keeping the ego away completely? Right now you have *You*, which is Spirit and *You* are the one who holds the key. The gates into the gap open differently for each person. Presently, individuals are learning about living in the present now moment and this marks the beginning of ego awareness. As you live from one now moment or millisecond to the next one you begin to feel your being of joy, peace and grace.

While you sit quietly with your eyes closed you may even say gently, out loud "I am peace, joy, love and grace." This statement may become a mantra for you as you feel one now millisecond and onto the next. As you meditate upon your mantra your *now energy muscle* becomes stronger. You are then able to slide into the next now millisecond and before you realize it you are ten to fifteen minutes into a deep meditation of just being who you are, which is peace in the moment. *Practice this now energy muscle* exercise and strengthen its muscular energy. Eventually, open your eyes and keep repeating your mantra. Notice how you feel with your eyes closed, then opened. You will arrive at a now energy muscular point where your eyes are *open* and you are stating your mantra, while still in peace.

The key for recognition *before* an ego thought arrives is for you to just continually be aware of ego thoughts and remember how you allow them to manifest. The deeper you are aware then the less you will need to be aware. It will just happen naturally for you! Then the gaps or the spaces between the ego thoughts become larger and your awareness will strengthen, therefore; there will be fewer ego thoughts.

Through practice of using the now muscle the *awareness energy muscle* strengthens and therefore eases the *unawareness energy muscle* which then becomes looser. Do you see dear reader how this works? You strengthen one muscle of awareness which then loosens or eases the unawareness muscle. This means you become deeply aware of ego due to the fact that you have strengthened your awareness muscle to a point that it unleashes the unawareness muscle. This then expands the gap before the ego based thought even arrives. This process also affects you physically through a rewiring of your brain synapses. There is no special, secret pill, drug or anything you can drink or eat, all you need to do is practice. This will do it! You have found the key. What will occur for you is the recognition that you have everything you require inside of you, already.

The next muscular step is most intriguing because what then happens is the deepened strength of your awareness muscle loosens. It loosens naturally when you realize that you no longer need to be aware of ego since you know there is no ego. Being aware no longer needs to occur as you are just living from a soft, natural, love or flow energy muscle. Which really isn't a muscle but an energy of pure love.

A question arises, is there a shortcut to eliminating the ego? The short cut is discovered through your moment by moment practice. The true self is a vastness, like a void. The original self has no mind, only consciousness. Therefore, there's no mind or thoughts, only joy and indeed joy is not a thought, it is a way of being and existing, nothing more than this. It is just you *being in-joy*. There is no English language to describe this feeling of joy or being. If you are a being of joy, grace, peace, stillness and happiness then you are living from heart and nothing more.

You may say, "I feel joyful today" and this energy is stemming from your being or beingness. The switch is moving from thinking first then feeling second, to now feeling first **then** thinking second. When you are living from a place of ego *freeness* or freedom from the ego, your thoughts of anything that is ego based disappear and only the gap of Light resides. This Light or energy then forms new thoughts or energy expressions, all of which are love, peace and Divinity. It is here when you discover all of life is originating from this eternal way of being which is simply an expression of self and self only. When you have fully and completely released ego beliefs, life does transform and change. As you read the Ego Curriculum Questions allow yourself to feel your answers and be open for the messages streaming from your inner self.

Ego Curriculum Questions

The following Ego Curriculum Questions will assist you in discovering who you truly are and what it means to be aware of ego beliefs. It is here within the recognition where you are which provides a smooth slide into grace. It is also important for you to not only read and ask yourself these questions listed below, but to share these with others, as well. Think about these questions and slowly begin to write or feel your answers. Move into your openness and allow yourself to just be aware.

Ego Curriculum Questions

1. What does ego mean to you? Is it external or internal?

2. What do ego thoughts say to you? Are these thoughts of grace and love or are these thoughts of destruction?

3. When and where do you hear these ego thoughts? What is their purpose?

4. If you hear an ego thought what do you do?

    a) Do you allow it to enter and move throughout yourself?

    b) Do you tell it to leave your body?

5. If you ask the ego based thought to leave, does it leave?

6. When an ego based thought leaves, do you feel better and more at peace when it dismantles and dissolves?

7. Are you able to say you can detect an ego thought when it arrives?

8. Are you able to keep ego thoughts away from you much easier than before?

9. Can you sense an ego thought just before it arrives? If yes, how do you know just before it arrives and are you aware of the tiny energy space gaps between the ego thoughts?

10. Can you make these gaps of space between the ego thoughts larger in vastness in order to keep the thoughts away from you?

11. What else are you aware of that is dismantling, changing or transitioning from your life?

Everything is in alignment with the energy matrix currently existing upon the planet. As you align yourself to Spirit of who you are already, you will be given all that you wish for and all that you have imagined and dreamed about. This is an era when everything is shifting and re-organizing. Embrace this beautiful time and all the transitions and recognize that everything is truly in perfect order and plan.

The Now Dismantling
Curriculum Section

○ Now Curriculum

○ Now Curriculum Questions

The Now Curriculum

F ully embrace the awareness of the now moment and move through this embrace. When you embrace the idea and the feeling of the now's exactness and then all of a sudden you shift away from this moment, that's when the ego is revealed. In other words, when you live in the now moment and lose it, you then begin to feel the emotion of pain and suffering. Expose this and tell this ego based emotion to leave since the ego will either be in the past or in the future, not in the present moment. Therefore, the exposure of the ego happens in order for the dismantling to follow. Many individuals have pushed through the stage of dismantling of the ego and are living from that place of all readiness or self-actualization.

The teachings of the *now* and being *aware* of the present now moment has been written about in several books and taught in workshops and at conferences. You may ask the question, what is being asked of you within the pages of this book? It is for you to consider that *the now no longer exists* because when you loosen the hold of ego the only thing left is your true Essence. Your Essence is all there is and it doesn't require any form of now, present time, since you no longer need the teachings of the now to discover and feel your Essence. The premise of the now curriculum teaching was to help you feel your peace, your Oneness to Spirit, your love and stillness, together, in *one single focussed millisecond*.

The whole idea concerning the Now Curriculum is to get you to feel for just one millisecond who you truly are. Once you loosen the hold of ego you are always in this state of feeling your Essence. You are then always present and nothing will take you back to an ego way of being and in fact you won't even think about it anymore. When this occurs you don't engage in even saying "ego is an illusion," since once you realize you are already self-actualized or enlightened your whole self switches and your life transforms. You no longer need to focus on the now moments to feel who you truly are because you are already there.

However, the teachings of the now moment is still required because we, as a whole planet or collective, have believed and perhaps even worshipped the ego for so many years that we now need to focus upon one moment at a time in order to feel peace. This scenario shows us the extent of ego based thoughts, ideas, opinions and behaviours we have allowed into our belief system. We now need to teach individuals how to live in the present now moment; one little moment at a time. This is now a common language and many meditations, yoga classes, other teachings have surrounded their practice around the present teaching of the *now*, even though this philosophy or idea of feeling your present now moment has been in existence for many years. It is just being placed into awareness over the past several years, consciously. The word awareness and being awake or awakened are included in the now teachings. One needs to be aware and awake in order to feel the present moment.

When you have awakened to the realization that you are already enlightened, Essence, Spirit, love and peace then you no longer need to focus upon the present now moment. Consider that every moment will be a now aware moment that you could name as All or Oneness. There will come a time when you won't need to take a meditation class to get back to peace because you will be a *walking peace* with no need for a structured way of finding this peace or stillness through meditation classes or alone. In fact you are a walking peace now!

The Key: Once you begin to realize and recognize that the ego is illusion and not real, you then no longer need to focus upon the now moment. You will live as your Essential Self every single moment and millisecond of your life and begin to realize everything differently. Frequently you hear people say "My ego keeps me grounded," but what really keeps you grounded is your physical form. One still needs to chop wood and carry water for daily activities such as eating, doing laundry and shopping for groceries. This is what is keeping you grounded and in fact you will begin to see the word grounded disappear from the English language, as it in itself is ego based. Just by being in your suit of body you are already grounded.

In truth there is no longer a now, this is exciting and wonderful. The energies or Spirit are supporting this truth and will maintain or hold energy space for all people to move into this way of being. By releasing the ego and living only from Essence/The Divine and recognizing that the now moments no longer need to be spoken about as you are now living as all or Oneness.

This way of living starts by making a slide step or a smooth step out of the now into The All which is the fullness of self brought about by embracing your Essence and discarding the ego. It is a step that is already waiting for you to just simply slide into its existence. There is nothing complicated here, no special effects that you need to achieve. All you have to do is believe in who you truly are, which is Spirit, simply in your human form, accessing love teachings through your form to share with others.

In essence and review; be carried along with the dismantling and dissolving steps of ego and the realization that the now is no longer necessary. Begin to explore the idea that perhaps the now will no longer exist after you realize that you are just *all* and no longer require the focussing of the now in order to feel peace. Once you have shifted through these steps of dismantling and dissolving you no longer need to live in the *focused now* moments because you then recognize that you are the open, vast, empty and enlightened. You no longer need to focus upon a minute millisecond moment as you *now know* you are this now moment of peace and stillness *all* the time or just *All*.

The following Now Curriculum questions ask specifically about your now. Feel and absorb the questions and answer in your truth with deep honesty streaming from your inner self.

The Now Curriculum Questions

1. What are you presently aware of now? Are you aware of where you are sitting? Are you aware of sounds, smells, sights, touches and tastes?

2. How are you feeling in the now present moment? Do you feel peaceful, serene and still? If not, then are you hearing any ego thoughts?

3. Are you engaged only in the now or in the past or future? Pay attention to where you are right now. Are you able to stay in the present now moment and for how long?

The last question is: how can you expand those moments to another now moment and be aware of this expansion process? You will no longer need to focus upon each and every now moment as you will be living the **all** and realizing that you don't need nor require the now focused moment in order to feel peace and stillness. This is illustrated in Figure 4 *The Now Curriculum (A)* where the first now millisecond is felt and depicted as a single now circle. The next now moment or millisecond is felt and then followed by the next continuing now moment that is joined together. Until finally, your full day of now moments *shift* and slide into the larger circle of ONENESS, which is the new Mayan Calendar post-2012. As you explore the

NOW

illustration, follow the arrow ribbons as they slide you to the next step approaching the disappearance of the now focussed milliseconds. You will be joining the vast Oneness of All, Love, Light, Ascension and open to your Essence. Expanded until the now disappears and you are aware each and every day.

You realize that the now when expanded is the Light. Which means, the now no longer exists and the Light is who you are, expanded from the still point of existence. This still point of existence is the place where you reside next in the now moment existence. It is a most incredible way of being and existing. When you place your self within the Light or place of peace you discover *you* – Spirit.

*When you awaken to ego as illusion, you no longer need to focus upon a now moment as you now know you are this now moment of peace and stillness **all** the time or just **All**.*

The Now Curriculum (A)
(Figure 4)

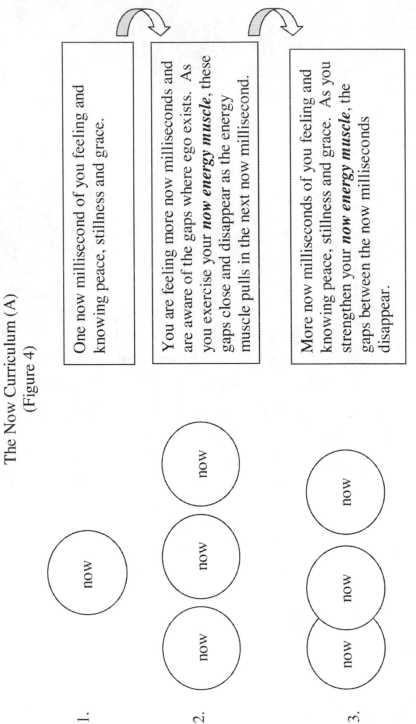

1. One now millisecond of you feeling and knowing peace, stillness and grace.

2. You are feeling more now milliseconds and are aware of the gaps where ego exists. As you exercise your *now energy muscle*, these gaps close and disappear as the energy muscle pulls in the next now millisecond.

3. More now milliseconds of you feeling and knowing peace, stillness and grace. As you strengthen your *now energy muscle*, the gaps between the now milliseconds disappear.

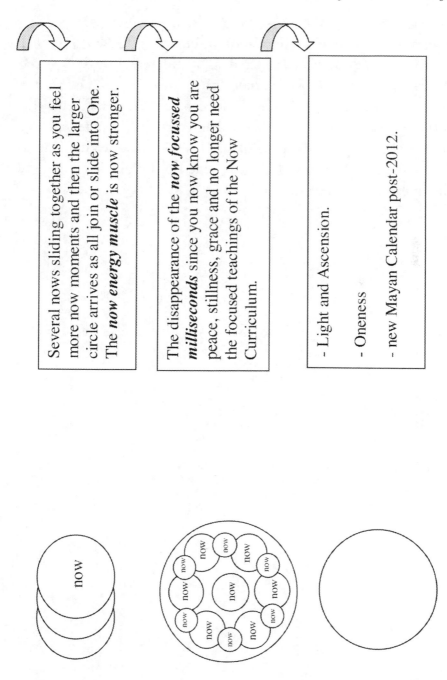

4.

Several nows sliding together as you feel more now moments and then the larger circle arrives as all join or slide into One. The *now energy muscle* is now stronger.

5.

The disappearance of the *now focussed milliseconds* since you now know you are peace, stillness, grace and no longer need the focused teachings of the Now Curriculum.

6.

- Light and Ascension.

- Oneness

- new Mayan Calendar post-2012.

In addition to Figure 4 *The Now Curriculum (A)* diagram, here is another illustration in Figure 5 *The Now Curriculum (B)* to be considered as a different visual description of this same expansion. The now is expanding through the **now muscle** from the central inner core of the now moment. This is the ascension into ONENESS which represents the outer circle or the new Mayan Calendar post-2012. This is just another diagram to illustrate the shifting towards the Oneness or Original Self and the disappearance of the now.

The Now Curriculum (B)

(Figure 5)

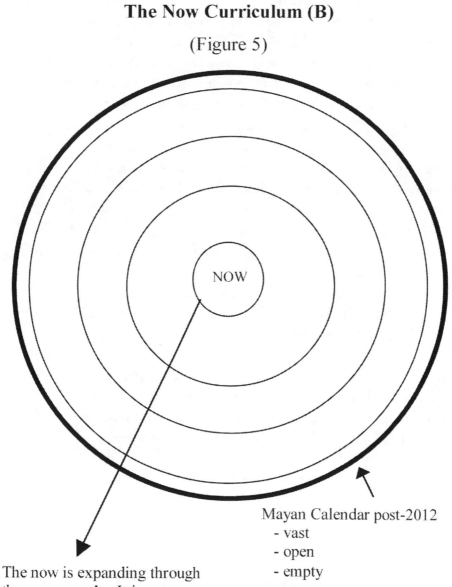

Mayan Calendar post-2012
- vast
- open
- empty

The now is expanding through the *now muscle*. It is an expansion or ascension into the Oneness – the Original Self.

When you live in the now you begin to realize that grace *and* ego dissolve as One since there are no dualities or polarities, *All* is *One*. The new revealed Mayan Calendar illustrates this by the simple circle. This circle is empty with only clear crystal energies amidst its core and nothing more than this. It speaks about how we are all moving into our Original Self, our Oneness to self and others.

Therefore, the future is gone and no longer exists because you enter into the nothingness, the emptiness and the vastness of the All. There is no language in any language to describe this All, yet language is presently the format that is used on the planet, for now. There will come a point in time when language will change completely and different forms will arrive due to the fact that all ego based terminology will dissolve. The dissolving energy appears much like a swirl or spin and could be called an energy swirl or some label it as a vortex.

This swirling of energy is a new energy that is assisting in the larger energetic shift on the planet. You may, at times, feel a bit dizzy or swirly yourself, maybe lose time, forget appointments or even forget what day it is. Time and ego are being dismantled which means everything is moving back to the simplicity of being, which is a slide step into the greater All. This is a swirl of energy that is existing in order to shift people into who they are already, which is peace. Enjoy and relax in the swirl and allow it to dismantle you slowly and gently.

> ***Be Love For This***
> ***Is Who***
> ***You***
> ***Are All Ready***

Woven throughout these next chapters are the below fifty dismantlings, including their results. Each touches upon the daily living aspects of career, relationships, finance, emotions, physical well-being, the mind, Spirit, and a sense of community. They speak directly to every one of us regarding the dismantling and dissolving of the ego.

1. There is no disease (dis-ease), only ease.

2. There is no pain or suffering, only love.

3. You begin to live in cooperation with the community and Oneness of all.

4. No more wars, abuse, self-sabotage and greed, only peace.

5. People recognizing they are White Light, Love and Spirit.

6. Parenting skills become gentle and loving without ego or fear.

7. Authentic selves of people resonate throughout the planet. In fact, you begin to recognize that even the word authentic is no longer required as it may indicate separateness.

8. Mother Earth and Father Sky are completely clear and clean of pollution.

9. An accepted wholeness of food and an organic way of living.

10. Music becomes simply Divine and joyous with messages of love.

11. No conflict, dualism or polarities. Everyone is recognized as Oneness with **all**.

12. Past life experiences are no longer relevant since there will be nothing to remember, think or feel about in the present way of living. There will be no triggers or memories linked to any past life or lives.

13. **All** people recognize the others **isness** or beauty and being.

14. Hope does not exist. You don't need to think of hope because hope means *a **better** **tomorrow*** and today is the day you have in every now moment, so be happy now in this moment. Read further into this book for more details about hope.

15. Realizing that everything is already and All Ready manifested for you.

16. The belief that we need to go through suffering to get to the White Light no longer holds true.

17. Nothing is based on fear, only love. Fear is gone.

18. Simplicity of life exists naturally.

19. Taking care of your body physically, emotionally, mindfully and spiritually.

20. Guided action originates from the heart and intuition, not from the intellect or ego based thoughts.

21. Everything is transparent and truly natural, where truth and honesty reigns.

22. All theories, belief systems, ideas, allowances and even knowings reshape themselves.

23. Countries will no longer be governed by laws and rules, but will shift in accordance with keeping peace.

24. Ego terminology shifts and changes to the language of love. The words "**ego is an illusion**" will no longer be relevant because it labels the ego, thus giving it energy.

25. Recognition that synchronicities don't exist since everything is just occurring through love and that is all, as every single millisecond is synchronized to the next millisecond through love.

26. Time becomes an illusion.

27. Medicine, school systems, technology, businesses, companies, social media, financial institutions and others shift, dismantle, dissolve and harmonize through peace.

28. People will naturally gravitate in the direction of love and make their next life steps while no longer feeling stuck.

29. You recognize that you are prayer, you are meditation, you are God, you are The One Creator. Since you **are** God, **you** don't co-create as you are the Creator. More details of this concept in the following chapters.

30. Re-writing of the soul's contract to initiate a contract filled with love and peace.

31. The old story of childhood pain is dismantled.

32. No need to read self-help or self-growth books as you are that **Being All Ready** and you realize there's nothing to do. Your purchased books on happiness are no longer required as this is who you are and you know, feel and believe this.

33. You realize that you no longer need affirmations since you are **all ready** or already affirmed as love and Spirit.

34. You no longer need to move through the darkness to get to the Light. You no longer need to go through the dark night of the soul to know you are Light because you are Light already and ready to live as Light.

35. You no longer think of anything that is ego based since you are the purity of Light.

36. Attachments to person, place or ideas are gone and you know that you own nothing.

37. You are one synchronized Being.

38. You are the Archangels, Guides, Angels, White Light – you are All.

39. No need for talk therapy or the therapeutic process as you have loosened the hold of your old pain-filled story.

40. You move confidently and fearlessly in all that you do, because there is no fear, there is only love.

41. No need to *forgive* only to *give forth love*. There is no betrayal, only the old stories that you signed up for before your Spirit entered the human body. These stories can now be released.

42. The worrisome feeling that one must be beautiful and young will disappear. No need for cosmetic surgery and in fact you will arrive at a place where beauty will have a new meaning.

43. Old theories, ideas, philosophies all built upon fear and ego will dismantle.

44. Nothing new needs to be created as it is already here!

45. There is no unconscious or subconscious since there is no ego old story.

46. You will no longer need spas, yoga and meditation classes.

47. No need for any type of relationship as you will feel whole and complete as yourself.

48. Retirement homes will begin to disintegrate as individuals will no longer believe in age, dis-ease and limits.

49. Dietary food intake will re-arrange and dismantle and you will eat only love, not fear. Meaning food that *feeds* your body love.

50. Eventually you begin to realize that *now* no longer exists, there is only All.

The above dismantlings and results are just a small sampling that have been sewn throughout the dismantling sections. Note each section contains several dismantlings. Allow yourself to tenderly be aware of your thoughts and feelings as you absorb each word within the messages.

Part III

The Dismantlings

You feel wonderful when in nature because nature has no ego and is transparent in love.

Dismantling the Inner Self

This first discussion deals with the dismantling of ego beliefs and the reframing of your inner self. Inside of *your self* what are you aware of that is being readjusted, transitioned or shifted? Are you beginning to ask the questions: "What is my passion? Who is my authentic self? What is my soul's purpose?" These questions precipitate the dismantling and dissolving of the old ego structure into the new consciousness. Simply stated, you are beginning to sense ego beliefs that you have allowed to influence you, which are all false and illusionary. You may be just starting to feel a pressure or the illusion of pain, suffering, an emptiness, loneliness and restlessness and you are now questioning: "How can I be happy and no longer have worries and anxiety attacks caused by fear?"

You are living in a time of self recognition and of knowing about these feelings of pain and now wanting to do something about this situation. We are entering an era of reconciliation, of giving love and peace to your self. Therefore surrendering to who you are *already*, which is peace, love and joy. If you can't imagine or even just allow yourself to be who you are, then who will? You are the Source or White Light expressing or reflecting itself through your human form; you are unlimited in love and joy to all. Your mind cannot understand nor reason what all this means. As a result, you are required to step beyond the mind, beyond fear, beyond everything. The lyrics in the song *"Beyond"* as performed by Tina Turner states that one must go beyond fear and into the journey within your self.

Beyond

"Go Beyond fear,
Beyond means to feel yourself,
Go beyond the rights and wrongs,
Go beyond to feel the Oneness of the unity."

(Turner, Tina. *Beyond Buddhist and Christian Prayers.*
Santa Fe, USA. New Earth Records. 2010.)

As you transition into your **love self** you may wish to start a personal spiritual practice, such as a gentle meditation in the morning, yoga or read special passages in books before the day begins or as it ends. Request for White Light/God counsel to seek answers or messages about your next step into your authentic loving and peaceful self. Are you familiar with the phrase, "the peace that passes all understanding," which really means peace moves through or gently passes all understanding? Where there is peace you don't need understanding and you don't require attachments. Where there is peace there is no fear. Where there is love there is no fear. Peace and love are inseparable from the depths of your Being.

You are Spirit within a coat called human, similar to a tiny blade of grass, which is Spirit covered in a little jacket of green. Your authentic self or White Light Being is always happy, so step into your happiness and feel this. Even if you are unable to feel this happiness discover just one activity that helps you feel happy. When you feel the happiness of doing this activity, then feel it more deeply. Your source of happiness could involve eating a beautiful, large strawberry or walking alone quietly at night. If happiness is what you are seeking then these exercises will work for you since you are saying to the universe, "I am transitioning away from ego beliefs into grace, into who I already am," "I am already happy, filled with love, grace and peace."

Be aware that when you shift away from happiness you are in fact shifting away from self, Spirit or you. You will then learn and be placed in many singular lines of lessons and possibly become filled with suffering and pain. When you believe in pain and suffering flat lines occur in your life which signals the beginning thoughts and feelings from your heart, questioning what is my purpose, who am I? Once you realize that you are Spirit first form secondary, you will discover that happiness and purpose is already within you and there is no need to seek it. Furthermore, there is no need to acquire anything from anywhere or anyone since you have already found your sense of happiness, within. You see, happiness is the key to what you and all people are looking for and in fact when one discovers happiness you may not even believe it to be true.

You may even sabotage or create a situation where you are believing that perhaps you don't deserve nor do you believe you are able to maintain this happiness. When you believe this then the happiness is pushed down. However, it is always there, you are the one who blocks this, nobody else but you. Your Spirit self simply waits for you to change your mind, so when this happens just rest and breathe in the beauty of the sunrise.

As you move away from ego beliefs you arrive in the alignment to happiness or your inner self, not just intellectually understanding what peace means. When you reach this state of realization you then realize that you are happiness. Do you see how this works? If you begin to think that you are unhappy, you then seek happiness and believe the ego's teachings and further illusions. For example, if you attain wealth and create a life filled with material possessions you may believe this will make you happy.

However, you then begin to slide more deeply into unhappiness and create more of what you don't want. Resurfacing once again, you release yourself of the material possessions and re-establish a pure form of happiness. When you opt-out of the illusion that happiness is material wealth, you realize you are already free, whole and happy. You proceed upon this higher vibrational pathway, and never look back as you know this is who you are. You are Spirit. You begin to forget that old way of existing from unhappiness and live only from the truth of joy.

There will be the realization that you own nothing and are therefore attached to nothing, this is true happiness. The need to own and attach is an ego based belief. Just simply live as an ***unattached love being***! Through this true way of living you then place your physical form within the natural state of being One, with all of nature. Nature *is* a natural elegance and this is where everything exists. Remember, you are the energy or Source that opens a blossom and reshapes the sky. Therefore the essence of the existence of everything in life is felt through your senses, through seeing, touching and hearing as in all of nature. How do you feel when you walk in nature or stroll along the beach? Are you opening all of your inner senses to feel all that nature speaks? Nature speaks through gentle, flowing ways as it whispers messages to the small grains of sand, as each sand grain tenderly touches the next through the rolling movement of the ocean's waves. Listen and feel the message of love, trust, peace and flow with what these grains are trying to communicate to you.

Know that each grain of sand is moving and shifting in perfect order. It is doing exactly what it should be doing and in fact it is just being done. The grain of sand appears to be hanging out or in with the waves and feeling its connected message of trust, all in the flow of life, that's all it knows. Listen to these grains of sand and allow them to soak into your listening ***spiritual ear***. Your listening spiritual ear is the way you hear the sand's gentle movement. Perhaps you physically draw close to the grains of sand so to feel their movement sift between your fingers. The spiritual ear listens to your intuitive, spiritual self. This means that you are listening with all of your senses in order to feel, hear, taste, touch, and smell. All of these combined senses create the all encompassing listening spiritual ear, eye, spiritual tasting and smelling. When you are listening to the small grains of moving sand what do you hear, what are you aware of and what do you feel? At this point you are probably sensing the joy and the fluidity of these grains, as well as their love and trust, that all is OK.

These whispers from the grains of sand can also be heard in the rustling of the vibrant coloured autumn leaves as they collect on one glorious tree, which embodies Spirit. Each tree has its own identity, and its own way of being, speaking or communicating with other beings, all through Spirit. These rustling leaves of autumn trees are simply whispering their messages to you and may be heard through not just one but all of your senses.

If you are walking through the forest and hear the rustling of leaves of multicolours, stop and listen to what they are saying to you. They have so much to communicate and present to you. They may in fact be saying, "Look at us, how beautifully we are swaying and rustling, as we swirl in the twists of the wind," "Listen to our message of flowing, being carefree and open to the gusts of wind blowing its breath of life in our direction." Arrive here in this language of the forest and listen to the subtle messages of love, trust, joy and complete openness.

During the spring, summer and winter seasons, trees may have a different message or the same message. Stop, listen and feel what their message is telling you. It is important for you to listen to the Spirits of nature for they are pure wisdom, clarity of Spirit, love, joy, peace and passion. This is all they know. When living from this place of nature's messages you allow the realization that everything is all ready created for you. Your life that was built upon ego teachings is no longer remembered when you allow your Spirit to shine. Instead of blockages, look through the possibilities. Time to hug a tree and feel its messages.

Dismantling the Self-Help/ Self-Growth Book Shelves

Over the past number of years the feelings of happiness, peace and joy have been captured in words which appear in books on the self-help/self-growth shelves in various book stores. Verbal labels have become externally attached to who you are *on a shelf* instead of an internal feeling. Simply stated, the feeling *happy* is now in several book stores on the shelf with book titles like "How to Become Happy," "What is Happiness?" or even "Steps to Become Peace-Filled," "How to Find Joy." Once happiness developed as a concept then words separated you from happiness and it became identified as something you needed to achieve.

So now we are required to enrol in courses, attend conferences, and purchase books to educate us to rediscover who we are already. But grace, love and Spirit are saying, "You are already this and are All Ready and nothing other than this!" You have just believed that you are not happy by believing ego thoughts. As a result, we are now wanting these books, more than ever, because the self-growth words need to assist you in coming back to your Original Self or ego free being. Yet realize that:

You are already where you need to be → Love.
There is nothing to do → just be.
The word self-growth → nothing needs to grow.

As the ego naturally dismantles from each person, relationship, business, financial institution and others, **then** people will search for a deeper meaning to life. This is when the truest peace of each person is revealed. Therefore the self-growth industry will flourish over the next number of years due to the ego dismantling. An assortment of self-growth books will become extremely popular. These self-growth book titles need to state ***you are happy already.*** In fact, on the front cover of each book should have a standard line that indicates "don't buy this book because you are happy already" or "don't buy this book since you are at peace already."

At some point, books that indicate "How to Become Enlightened" will also no longer be relevant because as you awaken you begin to recognize that you *are* already enlightened and there is nothing to achieve. Ego wants you to believe that you need to seek solutions externally of your self in order to find happiness, joy and enlightenment. Unhappiness is created by being out of alignment with the now and ego can never be in alignment with the present moment. The primary cause of unhappiness is never the actual situation, but your thoughts about it. Really, you don't have to work so hard to be happy. Life becomes easier when you renounce fear, suffering, emotional drama and accept happiness, love and peace.

*Treat yourself as **love**.*

Dismantling Fear

Everything that is based upon fear and not love is being dismantled. It is crystal clear as that, nothing more and nothing less. If you only live from fear then the energy of grace will slowly nudge its way into your awareness. Some people are living so strictly and thickly by fear alone that the moving of grace and the dismantling of the ego may be a touch more than a slight nudge. Nudging may occur until they feel and recognize ego. When you recognize ego, grace is able to slide into this space, which was once filled with ego. It is also suggested that the individual be open to receiving grace and love and to accept this gift.

If you believe in ego then it enters you through your open invitation, or if you believe in ego it will invite itself in and you will then open the door, according to your belief. But if you don't believe ego then it won't invite itself in and the door is quiet, with no ego knocking. The ego attempts to create fears and these fears create knots, you will need to *fear not* and rid yourself of these *fear knots*. The ego feeds on these fear knots as these knots tend to believe in themselves and create more of the same, they are self-perpetuating. For example, if you have intestinal difficulties or forms of digestive problems then the worry of this pain creates more fear knots and this becomes a domino or sequence effect. Be aware of how the feeding of the ego works? Stop believing the ego as the belief itself will be the invitation, however the invitation has an RSVP which is to *love* not fear.

You are love, not fear.
Whatever you fear is waiting around the corner because
you believe it to be true and are focusing on it.
Stress is just fear – it's that simple.

Where there is LOVE there is no fear.
Where there is LOVE there is no:

War

Doubt

Impatience

Disrespect

Abuse

Resistance

Hatred

Limitations

Self-sabatoge

Self-defeat

Where there is LOVE there is Eternal:

Patience

Respect

Tenderness

Happiness

Passion

Compassion

Knowing

Allowing

Trust

Today is a new beginning gifted to you. This day is a day to begin to realize everything is in perfect order – no worries – no fears – it just is! Never forget, just being is fun and exhilarating. It is time to hand over all thought forms of fear to the wings of the angels and gently step onto a peaceful, journey's path.

Upon your journey:
Rid yourself and surrender everything.
Shed all resistance and live only from gratitude.
Allow Spirit to move through you as this is
who you are already and All Ready.

Read the following questions about fear and feel what is occurring inside of you.

1. What do you fear?

2. Have you attached yourself *to* fear?

3. If you have dismantled fear are you fearful that it will return? Are you attached to this fear of returning?

4. Can Spirit move through fear and therefore can Spirit live and move through attachment to an illusion?

5. Is it true that you are the purest of love? If yes, then you are not fear, only love! This is truth as felt and believed by you.

• As you *feel* your answers to the above questions begin to explore attachment and detachment and what they mean to you. Attachment can be to a thought, emotion, material objects, relationships, food, alcohol, money, abandonment, death, vulnerability and to being lonely. Dear reader, remember that fear is false expectations appearing real or an illusion. Therefore, does this mean that if you find yourself attached to something, you are attached to an illusion? This illusion you have created to be real and it will manifest itself exactly what you are fear-filled about. For example, if you have attached yourself to the thought that you are not enough and have believed this to be true for many years, then you will continue to attract more of this illusion and manifest exactly that. It's what you don't want in your life. But this is an illusion, because you are enough, perfect, whole and complete. I sourced this quotation and feel that it relates to fear, safety and then to releasing: "When you take off your *armor* you then find and experience *amour*."

As you become more aware of ego and the dismantlings you then feel, see, hear, taste, touch and even smell attachments you have believed for years. These attachments may have been passed down from family generations of old, false, belief systems. For example, were you told by your mother, when you were nine years old, "You are just as shy as I was at your age." Now you are forty-nine and have believed this statement and therefore attached yourself to this false statement for forty years. To the point that certain life choices have been decided through this false belief, for instance, "I can't go to the party because I am too shy" or "I am too shy to talk to new people." You may even tell your child(ren) the same story, "You are just as shy as I was at your age." This old pain story continues to be taught and repeats itself for too many years and generations. Stop believing your old attachments and allow the dismantlings of these attachments to release from within.

If you intend to feel grace, love and joy then you will since you have placed your attention upon these feelings. The results, or that which you have manifested in life, will match your true intentions from deep inside. This means that the object, thought and feeling of your attention is your conscious choice. Various people's lives are lived through unconscious choices and intentions. Whatever you pay attention to, grows stronger in your life. When you stay steady and focus intensely upon what you love, then the ego dismantles. Once you place your *attention* on the *intention* of love and grace, you will then begin to feel and recognize that you are grace and love already. You will attract more of this into your life. This means you no longer need to place attention into the intention of being grace and love because you recognize and realize that this is just simply who you are – just *BE*! Nothing more.

Think it.

Know it.

Believe it.

Allow it.

Feel it.

And it will happen.

And it already has All Ready happened.

Just accept it.

Dismantling Old Painful Stories

The ego attempts to stick or adhere to the lower vibrations of thoughts, opinions and emotions of old stories from childhood injuries, illness and other forms of pain. Ego will attach itself here only if you allow this. When every fearful thought absorbs your attention completely and you begin to be identified with the emotions, you are then in the grip of the ego. Feel the pain of the old childhood stories or the discomfort of certain thoughts, then stop and release these so that ego suffering doesn't attach itself or that you in turn don't attach yourself to it. The ego will try to attach itself anywhere possible, in order to feed into fear and pain. This makes ego illusion as we are not fear and pain. We are *collectively* and *consciously* sliding closer to this realization. To the point where eventually even feeling any type of pain or fear will no longer exist. But collectively we need to first become more aware of who we are.

Dismantling of ego is also occurring within the family of parenting and what this means is that the parents/guardians of children who are abusive and/or raise their children on fear are now being exposed. It is a great time to see how parents are now beginning to just recognize that perhaps their own fears and childhood pain-filled stories will not serve their children well. It is known that if people hurt others they were hurt too. As people individually awaken to who they truly are and recognize the illusion of the ego, they then will raise their children from this realized place of love, joy, passion and compassion. This is already beginning to occur as more people are realigning themselves to who they truly are, which is love. In fact, if you change the script of the main character of your story you then adjust everything, like magic and all the secondary characters will also start to change their script. When *you* change, your children change, because your messages have changed. Your relationships with your friends change and your relationship with you also changes. You decide what kind of message to deliver to others, which is only love.

Let's explore a little further. If you have come from a painful childhood background and still, as an adult are living this pain and suffering. Begin to recognize that this pain occurred many years ago and it is time to release the old story. This is not who you are, yet you experienced this for a reason and that reason may or may not reveal itself to you in this life time. In fact the identity in the brain wants reasons, but Spirit cannot reason. Feel the childhood pain and release it in grace, then the ego slowly leaves and is fragmented into dust which then dissolves.

The reason you may presently be living in pain and suffering is you may live in sabotage, anger, fear, addiction and hopelessness. This now precipitates you into finally deciding to figure out why you remain in this continued cycle of pain, which is the ego's plan. Through a therapeutic process you may discover you are believing an old pain-filled childhood story. So you begin to *back-engineer* the story, a term used by engineers, which means you dismantle these old pain-filled beliefs by exposing them, feeling them and releasing.

Then you *re-engineer* by rebuilding and recreating your life through love, peace and stillness. You recognize you have believed this old story for many years and now it's time to re-engineer and reconstruct. When you dismantle, you feel the story, release the story and realize you are no longer the story and become the seer of the story and now rebuild it. The ego wants you to hold onto the pain, the sorrow and live as victim and believe that you are getting the raw end of the deal or say, "How could this have happened to me?" For some, ego beliefs have been built to create a structure of safety, which of course is illusion. This may stem from childhood trauma or pain where the child needs to protect himself or herself and be safe from various situations. As you explore this, the releasing of old emotions of pain will occur, and you will let go of this story and proceed into the deeper peace of who you truly are. You will soften all aspects of your daily life while connecting to this deep inner peace.

The ego doesn't want you to feel peace in any situation. In fact, you may have signed up for this pain filled childhood situation in order to move through it to help others. You may ask yourself, "How may I teach others how to rid themselves of their belief in ego pain and recognize it is illusion?" You designed your own template to *go through*, therefore feel it and let it go so others will be encouraged to do the same. You may have experienced pain and betrayal in the past. Remember that we are Spirit living in a human form. Therefore if you signed-up before you slipped into the human form to experience pain and betrayal, then is this truly betrayal and pain? Or simply teachings, learning, loving, giving love to those who lowered their vibrations to meet you here on the planet to be a guide/teacher for you. Should you *forgive* or just simply *give forth love* to this situation or experience and move forward with gratitude and thankfulness. Is your soul's purpose to move through the childhood pain or betrayal and recognize that everything is in perfect plan and love? You may say: "Wait a minute, I was abused as a child and now I'm to believe it was illusion?" The releasing of the pain of this story is imperative. The ego wants you to hold onto the pain until you feel bitterness, revenge and are unforgiving. Was your soul's contract to sign up for this painful childhood story in order for you to move through it? How do you feel when you ask yourself the following questions?

1. Was the experiencing of ego pain part of my soul's contract?

2. Does ego believe it was abused?

3. Does ego recognize abuse?

4. Do I create ego?

Questions and more questions ... What is your truth? What is true for you? Is there a dark night of the soul? Or has this also been ego based to convince you that you need to live through a perceived dark part of life. The belief that the dark night of the soul is part of what one goes through to learn what they need to learn in order to spring forth in love and Light. Several books have been written about this process of moving through darkness to reach the Light.

Now presently, what is being stated is that perhaps you no longer need to move through the dark night of the soul because you are already Light. Where does that statement move inside of you? Does it *feel* true for you or not? What do you *believe* is true for you? This is the point from where you live. If you believe in the pain of your old story then pain and suffering will continue in your life. You still need to release this pain and allow yourself to feel who you truly are, which is love. If you believe that no matter what happened as a child it is over and the wonderful, next part of your life is now here to be enjoyed. Actually, old stories needed to be in place, in order to help you be aware and expose, dismantle and dissolve ego.

If you are attached to your old story, it remains with you until you release it. These attachments may include relationships, money, competition, intellectual attachments, attachments to fear, your house, car, job, success, social status and every facet of your life. Loosen the hold of these attachments as they are induced by fear or ego beliefs. Also consider letting go of your own comfort safe zone; you may be living here out of fear and fear alone. Explore, shift out of fear, relax and enjoy life. Maybe wear a different colour of clothing, travel to a far-away land, walk a different walking path, wake up earlier, eat only healthy foods, and speak-up. When you begin to reach out of your comfort zone what happens is that the energy doors of endless possibilities open up for you. Just see and feel the Light, even if it is a Light sliver or a sliver of Light under the closed door. Just feel, that is all you need to do right now!

The ego feeds into itself through fear and will just want you to remain wrapped up in fear, which is all illusion. Sure, you may physically feel an alarming, yet exciting feeling bubbling inside of you when you first shift out of your comfort zone. You may wonder, "What will people think if I wear lime green pants and how will I feel?" "What will people think if I speak my truth?" Just do it and feel it through and have fun! You may be pleasantly surprised as others may say to themselves how brave and wonderful she is to wear lime green pants. They may say, "Look how much laughter is streaming from his eyes as he speaks his truth." Always be open to the endless possibilities in life and love.

These times are times when *all things* and *everything* connected with ego will be and are presently being dismantled and dissolved. People will come to recognize their true full self and continue to travel upon their path of recognition. The ego may be originating from a hereditary background as stemming from your family and certain language that was used within your family, and further ancestry routes or branches within your family. For example, you may hear terms such as, "You are as stubborn as your grandfather and always will be like him!" or "You'll probably get breast cancer because your mother had it," and so many more. These are not only threatening but based upon ego and when believed these thoughts will then be manifested. Self-esteem is thinking about yourself, so choose new words to think about yourself, you have the freedom to think anything you want. Tell yourself how magnificent you are.

Think back to what you have been told and then believed that would create or manifest itself through ego based ideas. These thoughts are extremely important to *stop* before you program these old memes or false beliefs into the thoughts of your children or children's children. These old thoughts or memes, as termed by Richard Brody in his book *Virus of the Mind* (Brody, Richard. *Virus of the Mind*. California, USA. Hay House Publishing. 2009.), may have been a belief system within your family for many years and therefore created or manifested. Just be aware and be observant to everything around you and allow the loosening of the ego's hold as it naturally by you disassembles. If you believe the meme that you are in severe pain and will be in this pain for the rest of your life, then you will be. If you believe you are love, grace, peace, joy and happiness and that pain is an illusion, you then no longer identify your life as pain. You see if you are someone who states, "Ok, I know I will have arthritis by the time I'm forty-five since my mother and father were arthritic by that age," then it will manifest.

If you allow yourself to know and believe that you are simply love and nothing more, then you will experience freedom. If you believe and truly know that you are unworthy then you will only attract and manifest this. We can no longer do this! For we as a people now stand up and say we are **love**. This truly is the Age of Transparency, an age of revealing and revelations within the revealing.

Distortion of the truth always in all ways leads to conflict and suffering which is the illusion of self.

What you believe is what you manifest or create!

"Your life is totally dominated by the system of beliefs that you learned."
Don Miguel Ruiz (Toltec master)

"When living from excuses you life from ego."
Dr. Wayne Dyer (spiritual teacher)

Say:
"Why me?"
then
say
"Why?"
Then say nothing.
Caroline Myss (spiritual teacher)

Dismantling the Old Contract

Your soul's contract has placed you where you are now in this lifetime, it may be time for you to reshuffle and rewrite your contract if you are living from pain and suffering.

Just request it now to be rewritten as a pain-free,
White Light way of being without allowing
or believing ego teachings.
Just request and it shall be done since this is how
the energy shift is moving upon the planet.
Just request and live true from your inner self of love and Light.
That is all there is, just simply Light which is who you are.

The dismantling is a natural cause of The Being – of just being. How could there be anything more? As the reader you may be thinking and even having certain emotions around what you have read so far. You may even feel this book inviting itself into your life. You may also be feeling that you aren't quite ready yet to read this information and this is okay. Or you may be asking yourself, "Why wouldn't I want this kind of world that is ego free, illusion free and living from the reality that I *am* Spirit." Why wouldn't you want to live from grace, goodness and a world of peace, no hurtfulness, war, pain and suffering?

It is a time to speak up in peace, step up in decisions, be true, be of guided action flowing from your heart. No more complaining and slide step into the being of who you already are. You are All Ready to go! It is time to smoothly slide into who you are already, which is like walking from one room in your house into another room. ***Come Be With Me***, is what your Spirit is gently whispering to you. Be aware of ego and its perceived movements. It will try to convince you it is real, alive and give you what you need and require to be happy, external of self.

But what is real and what is illusion? The physical form, body, the heavier matter is an illusion as it will dissolve or dismantle, at some point in time. You are here on a holiday in this human form and using the human form as a tool or vessel for the Light to shine through to others, but the ego wants to make it more complicated. What is transpiring is that you are living during times where people are beginning to ask questions of soul's purpose, life meaning and learning how to be happy.

Presently you are at the beginning of the shift, so you would think! But what is really happening is the ***shift has already happened*** – the great shift of collective consciousness, the great New Mayan Calendar has already arrived or has all ready arrived and everybody is just catching up. To put it another way: The Being has already manifested the new way of living and is just gently moving or shifting all people into this energy. It has already happened and is allowing you, if you allow you, to enter into its arms of complete freedom. You may think these pages in this book speak of the future but everything is already here for you now. Every single everything is being dismantled and dissolved that has been allowed to be governed by ego. Just be aware of the glorious way of these changes and shifts and know your truth. You have nothing to do, you are being done! We are all being evolved according to the order of the Natural World.

When you loosen the ego ideas and discard them then the space is filled with grace and in fact ***grace has always been there***, so perhaps it just slides over to fill that now empty space. Thus your new

Soul's contract is comprised of freedom, grace, love, joy, passion and compassion for all. It has been re-negotiated, without ego influence and re-aligned, re-signed and re-newed by you. Just by requesting this new contract, which by the way is just another way to say, *"I am love,"* has arrived now for you.

Be prepared, and when you recognize that the ego is illusion, this recognition stops the painful story *before* it happens. Therefore, your soul's contract is no longer necessary and in fact, before you enter the human form, you have chosen your parents and have reserved a human body and life. But what is now being stated is that you can now choose anybody as parent before you enter human form. It really won't matter since the veil between matter and Spirit is thinning. So what does this mean? You are loosening, dismantling and dissolving old pains, sufferings and ideas.

As you experience this, the Homo-Luminous form of energy begins to expose itself more, which means a thinning of old ego beliefs begins to take place. When this happens, if you decide to reincarnate into a human form again, you won't need to high-five an agreement with anybody before you arrive into human form since you will no longer need to learn what you need to learn, because there will be no pain, karma, suffering, blame or disharmony, only love. In other words, we have high-fived people whom we agreed to meet on the planet in order for them to teach us lessons and for us to teach them, as well. But what is being stated here, is that this will no longer be necessary since all will be love without karma cleansing or lessons being learned in order to live your dharma.

Therefore, the concept of karma will no longer exist as there will be nothing to clear and dissolve since you are now living in the now. All you do is live from love or you could continue to call this dharma. The term karma was used during a time when it was needed and indicated that one must clear the karma in order to move into their dharma, this is presently being freely dismantled, reshuffled and dissolved. There are new humans being born on the planet who are karma free or they can be referred to as Rainbow Children or whatever term you wish to describe these children who have no belief in ego. They are Children of the Light or Light Beings and live only from love, peace and a deep knowing.

The arrival or realizing that you are love is the belly of soul's purpose. Furthermore, you begin to feel there is no soul's purpose and not even purpose, only soul which is love. Nature exhibits this beautifully as it is naturally in alignment with Spirit and love. Appreciate the leaves on the forests' floor, the birds swaying in the trees, the ants crawling through the Mother Earth's soil and the animals quietly sauntering through the forest. This is nature's display of the flow of love. All of these creatures have a trust that everything is in perfect order and alignment. Every day of their lives these living creatures, even rocks and minerals, experience a love for existing. When the creatures of nature move and shift through life effortlessly and manifest what they need, then you know it ***knows*** and ***believes*** it is love and peace. This knowing could be called purpose or reason but not intellectually from mind, only from a natural existence.

What would a tree be without its leaves? It would surely die as the sun is absorbed through the leaves to gift it its food, which ensures it survival. How would the soil nurture itself without leaves decaying on its earthen floor? What would birds do if they didn't have the branches on the trees to sit upon or the squirrels to jump limb from limb? Trees, their leaves and branches are most needed in our forests and on this planet. What would the forest do without its bees and butterflies? The forest requires these insects to assist in the pollination of plants. The pollination is required in order for the plants to continue their reproduction cycle or regermination. Insects actually have an extremely important duty to fulfill. Without these insects, we as humans would not have the brilliant flowers, trees, even the spectacular weeds to enjoy. The animals would not have a place to live or create a habitat. Each of these nature creations have a natural existence, it just does what it does to create balance and harmony. It is within this balance and harmony where peace resides.

Allow *allowance* to take you over and *believing* to rest in your bosom. Allow a knowing to fill you up in all areas of your self. Be comfortable with who you are and be akin to the leaves on the forest's floor. They live on the trees for a certain length of time, until the tree decides to hibernate or until the leaf decides it is ready to fall to Mother Earth's belly. Once this has been decided by Source then all is in place for the leaf to fulfill its duty, as a leaf. Now as it softly falls to the ground it becomes a decayed, wonderful form of dust. In turn, it enriches the soil for other trees and plants to begin their growth cycle. The leaf just flows into its destiny with no resistance from leaf to dust.

No fears, no worries, everything is in perfect plan just for you. Trust the universe. Know, believe, and allow its fullness and embellishment to move through you since you are the universe. Allow your self to live naturally, as if you already know, believe and allow the Light to shine through you. Similar to the leaves of the trees and the insects and the animals in their natural habitat, they just live. They didn't really require a self-help book to convince them of the idea that they are love as they already know this. No deep thinking was involved, just allowing, nothing more than this.

Have you ever noticed a small snail? Within the swirl or spiral designed circular shell, inhabits a petite being. A being that is filled with the Creator, White Light, trust and a deep knowing. Since it is small and at times unseen one may think it is insignificant and unworthy. Some individuals may feel small, invisible and unworthy and they then create a protective shell around them, just like a snail. However, learn from the snail as it lives its life fully, to the best of its own ability. It even carries its simple life with it where ever it travels or sojourns. The little snail goes about its day to day living without any form of material stuff to carry around. All it needs to do is sleep inside its mobile home, then go for a bit of a walk with its attached home and eat small meals. The snail makes the best of its life and wants nothing more, it is content and strong in its belief of life. A tiny being with a love to exist and to show others the meaning of the *flowing* in life and trusting that all is in perfect order. Every morning when he/she awakens the snail brings gratitude to the universe. It is grateful to live for another day with more moments to absorb. Walking with its home and eager to explore the new territory on the belly of Mother Earth.

It is through the teachings of these creatures that allows humans to see, feel, touch and taste life fully, to the best of ones ability, to live moment by moment. The little shell creature may only live for one more moment or thirty seconds as it may be eaten by a hungry bird or a small animal. All it knows is that it has *this* moment and maybe more. It opens its awareness up every morning and feels and knows this is another day filled with moments in which to feed and live upon. The snail says to itself, "I will slowly move forward and begin my day by existing in my mobile home. I'll eat my daily food, walk my daily walk and be a role model for others, even though I am little, I am filled with the Spirit of strength, purpose and meaning. Humans will watch me as I slowly flow with life, with the universe and notice how I trust that everything is in perfect order. Nothing is out of place."

"If I live for this moment then die in the next I know I have fulfilled my purpose. I know that I am in perfect alignment. So I do my best, I try my hardest, to the best of my ability from now until forever." This is a lesson from the little shell creature for all humans. Nothing more needs to be explained. Be consciously aware and no matter what you have signed up for through your contract, surrender into this moment of existence and be here in this place. There is no other place to be but here and now.

Dismantling Polarities

T his section delves into the dismantling of the concept of polarities. Polarities is an interesting **One** as it involves opposites, conflicts and two, yin yang which are considered to be necessary in order to create balance. Ancient philosophies, science, religion, astrology and various other disciplines factor into this concept. In other words, opposites exist to create a sense of completeness, however, this will no longer be true. The ego continually wants to create opposites, conflicts and polarities. Presently upon the planet the entry of Oneness is emerging, everyone is beginning to be connected to eachother, with no exceptions.

What this means is that war will no longer be valid as the opposite of love can no longer exist; we cannot have war, killings, pain and suffering or ego. Yet, if we believe in polarities then this is what we will manifest. We have manifested wars, self-sabotage and hatred for too long and now is the time to just stop it. Even if you believe the idea that you can fight for peace you are once again using ego to create peace. This is impossible since ego does not recognize nor want peace. Peace attracts more peace! Speaking in the language of peace, stillness, love and joy brings with it the result of calmness, without any conflicts. Conflicts meaning one conflicts with one another which are defined as dualities or polarities. Just one person at a time living from their heart of love will stop the wars.

Let's explore the idea of polarities even further. The concept of polar opposites has always been considered necessary for balancing energies, ideas and thoughts. Yes, at one point this concept was important, that is not the case anymore. The new energy shift, upon the planet is moving in this energy of balance, it is all ready waiting for people to recognize and feel it. It is time to look inside yourself and discover if you have any conflict. If you recognize a conflict within then you are becoming aware of the attack of the ego. This attack may be considered the war within your own self or it may even be an act of self-sabotage, which is still an attack against your self.

The pain and suffering created by this inner war is all illusion and if you believe in this illusion *you* continue to create a war inside of yourself. Let go of the idea that you are meant to live with pain and suffering. Move forward into Knowing, Believing and Allowing that you are love and nothing more than this.

Polarities and polar opposites are defined as two and not working together or conflict. The illusion is that they create balance, which has been our common frame of reference, but this is no longer the case. Oneness is the only energy permeating through the Universe and slowly placing people back into their Original Self, which is the Oneness of Spirit. In my book *Movement of Stillness* I speak about the Oneness in great detail when revealing the new Mayan Calendar post-2012. The Mayan Calendar is an empty circle as everything within it is vast, open, allowing and is *All Ready*.

New Mayan
Calendar
Post-2012

You have arrived into an era where you will view people gathering together to help eachother. There will be individuals moving into a simpler way of existing, with organic foods becoming more popular, and money used for grace not for the purpose of greed. These changes represent the dismantling, reshifting and reshuffling of how we are living and where we as a grand planet of people, are shifting in a positive, specific direction.

The **balance is already here**. There are no polarities or polar opposites or conflicts since everything or **all** is balanced and One, yet the ego will have you believe differently. The ego wants you to believe that you need to have two or opposites to balance; you need male and female, white and dark, yin and yang, well no more. What you believe is what you will see and inevitably what you create.

When we were living in the Age of Pisces the polarities or opposites where characterized by two fish swimming in the opposite direction. Now we are living in the Age of Aquarius where water and the flow of water are shifting with gentle, easy movements. There's an openness present and the polarities are continuing to lose their energies. Water flows where there is least resistance and smoothes rocks until they have no sharp edges. In fact, the water doesn't concern itself with the rock it passes over. As water moves it dances with the direction of the rivers currents. Ask yourself if you are creating an unnecessary struggle by swimming against the natural currents of life? If you do flow against life then you are believing old ego thoughts that cause pain and suffering. Don't attempt to push the currents within the river, just let it be and flow.

This is also the age of believing that everything is already in perfect balance and that you can take that first step into what you truly want to do in this life time. Your paths will cross with more people learning how to accept other individual's ideas and thoughts that may be different (not opposite), from yours. We are transforming into a new, yet an old original species; this suggests an uprising of a purity of love which is triggering our spiritual growth, awareness or our remembering.

These are marvellous times to **be-living** upon the planet and **believing** in our planet and who we truly are, which is Spirit. We marvel when we see and hear people wanting to get along and connect, for it truly is a time of Oneness. Within each person this Oneness is revealing itself through different events and situations within their lives. People are coming to realize there is a Oneness, which is the true balance.

Perhaps this new way of living is too hippie granola, flip flops for you or too idealistic. Ask yourself, why would you continue to agree to live a life of conflict, hurt, pain and suffering? Why would you choose to live this way? If indeed you are experiencing a painful situation such as a death of a child, divorce, or dis-ease, then recognize and feel the pain. Allow it to wash through you, with no resistance. Release this pain into the water currents of the rivers of life. Know that this situation will flow, release, cleanse and shift as it needs to, be sure to just allow.

You may never understand the reasons why events occur because Spirit does not reason. If you do discover reason, you wish you had just been more trusting in the first place and allowed the currents to flow during the situation. Remember, everything is in perfect plan and order, nothing is out of step which means the balance is always here, there's no need to resist. When you trust that all is perfect, whole and complete then an immediate balance or peace is recognized and deeply felt. There is nothing to do, you are being done, shifted and gently flowing in the currents of life.

You are The Being, the One Creator, the river, the sunrise and the sunset. There are no polarities there is just the Oneness – The Original – The Being – Love. Once you genuinely feel this deeply you will experience such joy and peacefulness that you will never go back to living from an ego state of mind and belief system. In fact, you will discover there is no thinking involved, only being in the now. The mind is a place where all thoughts make themselves known to you. Are most of your thoughts your own or do they originate from various sources?

Most, if not all thoughts are not yours, but ego based. Once you recognize or observe an ego thought, it is then exposed and must leave as you have shone a light upon its darkness. The ego will then slip away through your energy of being consciously aware. Eventually, you will discover that all you need to do is recognize these ego thoughts of illusion of fear, self-doubt, low self-esteem, and self-sabotage and once recognized they will leave.

What you think about is what you will attract, even if it is an ego based belief system. The Law of Attraction will gift to you or mirror back to you whatever you think, believe, feel and ask for. However, even the Law of Attraction will begin to shift and dismantle. At some point the Law of Attraction will only attract back to you, goodness and only good thoughts. Any form of negativity will be repelled away from you. This means that The Law of Attraction will only recognize love and goodness.

When you begin to recognize negativity and suffering are illusions, this will **not** be attracted back to you as the collective planetary vibration's energy frequency will be high enough to slide away negativity. In other words, more individual's are remembering who they are, which is Spirit. The heart energy vibrating throughout the planet is the remembering that you are just love and thus stopping the ego. This is the energy that is shifting the Law of Attraction's energetic attraction back to you only love and goodness. Eventually the Law of Attraction will no longer exist as love will prevail and only love. Therefore the duty of the Law of Attraction becomes fulfilled.

Presently, everything you think, feel and believe *is a request* to the Universe. You have heard the phrase, "Be careful what you ask for." So how do you want to live? If you say, "I am unworthy, unloving and dislike myself," then the universe will provide this to confirm it for you as this is what you are asking for. Why not focus upon goodness, kind thoughts and loving ideas and this is what you will attract naturally, why wouldn't you do this?

A new consciousness has arrived upon the planet and is shifting everything. You need to know that everyone is being supported spiritually and energetically through this shift of consciousness. It is an energy that is here and now and is shifting everybody back to a place of stillness.

Begin to deeply feel who you truly are and know anything that is not of love is an unstable structure built from the illusion of ego. It was built, due to the fact that individual's believed it was real and would satisfy their own inner conflict, this is also an illusion. One illusion can create another illusion as you believe the first illusion to be real and powerful but both are not real. The more illusions you create, the larger is the ego structure, although it becomes weaker and therefore must dismantle. The ego structure is built with very weak, dust-like ego particles. Do you see how this works?

Perhaps you were born into a family whose premise it was to live from ego or greed. Also, it could be a large family-owned company that has been built upon this illusion. Surely this business structure will dismantle. Various departments or the business as a whole, or the family unit, experiencing disputes is no longer viable and held together or supported. This is all due to the weak ego material that formed the foundation of the business. Change the philosophy of the company to one of compassion, honesty, peace and harmony. Switch it up so that it operates from giving not greed.

A company whose philosophy promotes reflection time for its employees, breaks for nurturing one's self, building relationships and valuing employees, providing training for the employees by bringing in guest speakers on specific topics for employees, and more is vital to the overall grace being of the company. Now is the time for everything to change and shift into the realm of possibility.

The song *Imagine* as sung by John Lennon embraces the idea of imagining that we are all One with no separateness.

Imagine

"Imagine there's no heaven, it's easy if you try ...
No hell below us, above us only sky ...
No need to kill or die for and no religions too ...
Take my hand and join us ..."

(Lennon, John. *Imagine*. California, USA. Capitol Records. 1989.)

John Lennon knew that he wasn't the only one dreaming about a place of Oneness. He dreamed that all people would be joining hands, living in harmony within each person and with others, whether this meant in a family, friends or within a business environment. Now is the space and place to live this! Now is the time.

Dismantling Education
and Teaching Styles

Ego is also present within the education system. For example, the testing of students on a curriculum to determine their intelligence level stems from an ego, fear based belief. Children have spoken about their nervousness and have resorted to the shedding of tears concerning testing. This fear based method of teaching needs to stop. What is occurring within the education system is that ego is being taught through the controlling power of school systems. Which results in teachers attempting to be controlling as they too may be teaching from fear. They need their students to perform academically, in some cases to hold their teaching positions, reputation, keeping parents/guardians happy with academic performance, or to maintain funding money. This means that certain school systems require academic grades for operation.

Children are not only taught ego, fear based ideas at school but at home, as well. Some parents have stated that if their children achieve a certain grade they get rewarded. This is an example of an ego fear based way of living or ego gratification for external rewards. All of this is changing through the dismantling of ego fear based teaching and parenting. This dismantling is now occurring and will continue to occur over the next number of years. The ego is being taken out and a gentler, softer way of teaching is arriving and has actually arrived already in several places. There is a movement of several teachers who are now saying, "Enough is enough, our children need a social and an emotion based curriculum," and a Living School that focuses on everyday life skills.

The ego is also being dismantled from competition which is represented in school tests, sports, art, business and other areas. The ego will dismantle from these areas and you will begin to see the results within the school system. Losers and winners will no longer be the focal point and in its place what will be taught is the concept of heart connection to your self and helping others. Instead of competition, that is being encouraged, students will be taught the recognition that each person is complete just as they are, regardless if they are an A+ student or not. It won't make a difference if they play on the most popular winning football team or not. All are perfect. This type of curriculum will be taught in schools through a very natural evolution as people begin to recognize that a different way of teaching needs to be developed. In fact, grades such as A+ or an F and other designated special markers determining intellect or failure will dissolve.

Therefore, you will see a huge shift in the teachings of intellectual knowledge and testing in schools. These concepts will eventually slide into the work force and indeed this is transpiring already. It is a time when intellectual knowledge and information is dismantling and leaving in its place simply feelings and intuition. Educators will be teaching about feelings and how to feel your intuition. Further teachings will include "getting along with others" and living your true self. This means a renewed sense of honesty and to speak kindly to all people.

The new curriculum – free of ego – filled with compassion, love and gentleness, which happens naturally when you remove all intellectual reasoning. We are living during the time of the exposure of the new Mayan Calendar which has ushered in an entirely whole new energy that is naturally shifting into the heart and away from intellect. It is a time to only live in harmony and breathe from the heart and to teach the children how to do this, as well. Then what you will notice is that children actually carry inside of their hearts the new curriculum for the schools. They are here to help us teach them!

Dismantling Relationships

The illusion of the ego also moves through relationships. If you are involved in a relationship that is built upon each other's belief in ego teachings, then this relationship will indeed begin to shift and reshuffle itself into a very different form, or it may completely dissolve. The ego based relationship may be contingent upon the perception of status, money, possessions, reputation, achievements, success or even failure or no material possessions. Perhaps both of you feed into each other's ego belief system and are proud of the ego teachings of status and popularity or no popularity. But this relationship is all ego illusion, not from grace or love. You are in the relationship, but not living or breathing in this relationship, through love. A true relationship is one of absolute love, peace, joy, passion, compassion and greatness of grace. If this is not your relationship then a shifting may need to occur where the ego is shuffled away.

A planetary shift is occurring everywhere, therefore you may feel that something is realigning itself or changing in your relationship and within your self, as well. *Your self* is a combination of several selves that are defined as mind, body, Spirit, feeling, soul and energy. It is here in these selves where the ego is being *naturally* dismantled and indeed your grace is moving ego out instead of ego (edging grace out) pushing out grace.

These times of today are exciting and are truly allowing you to slowly shift back to your awareness of self. You may experience some pain within the shifting back to your awareness. Gently feel the pain, then gradually release one pain at a time and release it fully so there are no remnants remaining. When you shift out of pain what remains is your ***already or all ready*** foundation of Spirit or you, which has always been here. For some people there is no pain releasing, they may just experience a very powerful ***Ah ha! moment*** and they live from this moment on in love, as all old thoughts and patterns immediately melt away. This instant awakening is occurring more frequently for many people now.

When you recognize you are just love, you begin to feel differently and things that bothered you previously will no longer be an issue. Relationships and your view of the world will change dramatically. Not to mention your development of new ideas and thoughts, representing a loosening of the old childhood story and of course you begin to genuinely ask, "How may I serve and help others become aware of who they truly are?" You reach a place where you love very deeply. You fall in-love with you, as you are love and you renew the love for your self by displaying loving actions and by living in the present. When truly living from love you no longer need reasons to love someone, you don't even need to choose love since your true nature is to love. You also begin to dismantle the understanding of ***forgiveness***. Forgiveness now meaning: ***giving forth love*** to those who have hurt or injured you. Maybe you send them love and let them know they too are born of love.

The ego wants you to hold onto pain, hurt, betrayal and turn it into bitterness, revenge, hatred and deep feelings that God is against you. Are you entering relationships that are just simply an extension of your old story? When you loosen the hold of ego you begin to recognize that all people are love since you are Spirit first and form second. All people are created from the same energy or Source/White Light. All are One.

One must remember that we are all One in Oneness. It is a spiritual situation where you are able to attain a purity of one's relationship with oneself in order to have a relationship with others. Who you are and what you do and what you say influences everybody since all are connected to each another. The more in touch or awakened you are to the fact that you are already enlightened has an incredible impact on other people. It means that you are understanding, feeling, believing and allowing your true self to come forth and others will become part of this as they will also experience **this** emanating from you. It means for you to become open and free for you to realize your awakened self and to show others this truth, so they too realize and move into this awakened state of being.

It is a time when all people are needing to realize there is a greater power within each of us. This greater power will gently guide and keep you safe and warm no matter what relationship experience you are experiencing now or have experienced. Remember we are all Spirit in a vast open sea of energy. All helping and nudging eachother along our destiny's pathway, toward consciousness. We are not in competition with others, for there is no race. Some individuals have come back to the planet to help those to love and allow.

When you change, you then influence others around you since they feel your energy shifts and see your positive attitude. The song *Man in the Mirror* by Michael Jackson, messages that you start with yourself first as you gaze in the mirror. It is the person you see in the mirror that needs to believe who they truly are and this belief will assist others. When you are aware of ego beliefs you allow the change into believing who you really are.

Man in the Mirror

"I'm starting with the man in the mirror.
I'm asking him to change his ways ...
If you wanna make the world a better place
Take a look at yourself, and then make a change ..."

(Jackson, Michael. *Man in the Mirror.*
Toronto, Canada. Sony Music. 2003.)

Remember, that each person has a relationship experience with all people, not just with themselves. Each experience was required in order for the teachings of lessons from the soul to process living, learning, dismantling old patterns and removing old ideas. In the releasing you become fully real-eased which then transfers to a realized state of being. What this also means as you become more at-ease or real-eased you will also attract the same energetic way of living into your life. When you arrive in this place of being and greatness, it is from this place of Light where you begin to build your relationships. You create a transparent way of living and realize that you are an illuminated form which is simply Spirit, an instrument that is one for peace, kindness, gentleness and love.

Furthermore, your relationship with yourself is constantly reshaping and re-shifting your relationships with others. This is due, in fact until one believes and feels this truth and they are in turn able to flow with life. To clarify this, if you are one who believes and feels that life should never change, then you may experience pain and suffering because what is intertwined within the doing the same is an energy or belief in the fear of change. It is a fear that nothing can change since if it does you will not survive.

This is a false belief and in fact when you begin to feel and believe that all is perfect no matter what *then* and only then will you begin to live a life filled with bliss, happiness, calmness with no worries. This is the most beautiful journey you can live. But what doesn't change is your eternal Being of Spirit, it is always there, waiting, patient and true for you.

It is similar to the tides' waves that patiently await the return of the moon. The moon also patiently awaits its return to the canvas of the ocean. Its reflection is the paint as coloured by the brush of the sun's rays. Its movement of beauty is the tides shifts of the ocean's waves. Without these waves, in order for tides to change shape, then sea creatures would have difficulties shifting and transforming themselves and sourcing enough food to eat. The tides circulate and detoxify the bottom of the ocean. They stir things up, thus creating freshness and change. It's interesting how naturally and freely this occurs within the oceans with no grumblings from the local community of fish. No complaints from the whales of the outer seas and no *seamails* of concern from the gentle tender corals rooted deeply within the oceans floors. All is perfect and all is in alignment, and in relationship to each other. The sea community does not instruct the moon, telling it what to do and what not to do, according to their expectations. Everything is just working instinctively, within a perfect relationship. As stated by Don Miguel Ruiz in his book *Prayers* (Ruiz, Don Miguel. *Prayers*. California, USA. Amber – Allen Publishing. 2001.), "Can you respect your beloved so much that you never have to tell him how to be, what to be, what to believe, what not to believe? Can you love him so much that you never put restrictions on the expression of his life, on the expression of his Spirit?"

Simply allow love of who you are to shine forth to all people!

Dismantling of Business and Money

Another example the way ego is revealing and dismantling itself is through the shifting and removal or restructuring of the business environment. Businesses, whether a small private business or a large financial corporation, are being dismantled if they are built upon the shaky foundation of ego, which means the foundation stems from: greed, power, fraud, control, manipulation, revenge, and mistreatment of staff. Once again you see this transpiring today and everywhere and it seems to be starting within the financial institutions. What needs to happen is for institutions, agencies, all businesses to restructure and rebuild from peace and truth. Perhaps the entire structure of a specific business will be dismantled and dissolved. It may be the interior structure of specific departments or duties, roles, jobs, philosophy, management of staff, and controlling of money will be dismantled or it may only involve one specific job or role that is reshuffled and reorganized.

You are hearing more information about whistle blowers in companies, businesses, and agencies. Truths are being spoken and told within companies and to the media and some of these truths are being heard and some are not. After all, this is The Age of Transparency whereby everything is being exposed and shown. During this natural exposure the arms of grace will appear and capture the dismantling pieces. Grace is picking up the pieces of rubble and assisting in restructuring and rebuilding businesses, agencies and companies. As people are drawn down to their knees in the rubble they find grace. If they listen and be aware they are able to pull these pieces together and rebuild the business or their departments from this grace. Rebuilding, remodeling and reshuffling is vital in order for the fresh beginnings to arrive. It is no longer about money, power and control, but about how may I serve others? The truths are being revealed and more and more each day.

If you are presently experiencing a business restructuring just allow what needs to happen, happen. Bring in a **structural rehabilitation program** which means you need to create fresh new philosophies, ideas, meanings and respect. Your building materials are now fastened from grace not ego.

All institutions, agencies, and businesses built upon truth will expand and flourish since this is what they will attract, truth and honesty. Only ego will feed ego which means that ego does not feed grace, although ego appears to bring people to grace. You may ask, "Is ego working for grace, but just doesn't know it?" What is occurring, as stated previously, grace is pushing through the ego via The Being or The Being is saying enough of the ego, it is now time for its full exposure.

Ego does not have the capability to feel and know grace and love. Ego knows pain which needs to be first recognized in order to be revealed, felt, dismantled and dissolved. Then this space allows you to move forward in life to clearly make decisions from love, peace and joy, not greed, pain, fear and power.

Another interesting point to ponder is that ego is greedy for poverty. In other words, misery of poverty fulfills the ego's appetite for the abundance of poverty to justify a sense of victimization. Which can also mean that ego captures greed of money, for more money, as well as the greed of poverty. Therefore, if you are greedy in money rich, you believe the ego thought of living as a victim. This means one lives in a fear of losing everything, which is interpreted as greed. The flip-side is if you are greedy as poverty, you are also living in a fear-based victimization existence. Both are the same fear-based greed energy: needy, desperate, feeling not enough, helpless and victim. The two are the same because *you are still* allowing ego and ego moves between both of these beliefs.

Money is realigning within the energy shift. It will not have the same meaning and will in fact be so dismantled and dissolved that the ego way of using, manipulating and controlling money will disappear. You are already witnessing more money being used for goodness. The rallying of new energy monies is strongly coming forth. Furthermore, exchanging services without the use of material money will also become a new way of living and conducting business.

You may begin to recognize that you own nothing and when you give anything away, know that it wasn't yours in the first place. Become detached from everything and allow the flow to happen. You are giving *from* Source since you *are* Source.

Dismantling Technology

Technology that is characterized by its aggressiveness will also change due to the ego dismantling, and will be used for helping others in a genuine way. Greed, popularity, isolation and insulation of people on computers or sending information through the internet waves to hurt others will cease. There will be a recognition of the dangers of the electromagnetic fields created by the technology of iphones, ipods and computers. Ego has stuck or attached itself to and through technology. The dissolving of ego in this field is slowly occurring as more individuals become aware of the perceived environmental and human affected situations as created by electromagnetic fields and hurtful information being distributed by the internet system.

There will come a time when people will just simply begin to move or shift away from the technological world and slide into a simpler more organic way of living. As individuals awaken and become aware of this, you will see further shifts in social media. There will not be so many negative stories since people are starting to become more awakened and will speak kindly towards eachother and to all.

Dismantling Ideas Regarding Affirmations

This next dismantling encompasses the idea of affirmations. We have been taught that positive affirmations need to be stated in order to convince ourselves that we are happy, love, and peace. Yet this is who we are already. Keep in mind that all of our thoughts are affirmations. If you say, "I am unworthy, not enough and will never achieve what I wish to achieve," this will be affirmed. However if you state, "I am love, I am safe, I am peace," this will also be affirmed. Every thought, emotion and behaviour that is affirmed will happen, as the universe will give you what you request. If you have been stating specific affirmations such as, "I am love, I am peace, I am joy" begin to recognize that you are this already.

Ego wants you to believe you are not love, joy and peace. If you believe this to be true then you have to repeat certain affirmations to confirm that you are love, joy and peace. Then it becomes important to focus upon the now moment and state a positive affirmation.

It is a time to stay focussed upon who you truly are and rest assured life does simply dance in ease since this is your true self: *just-ease* and nothing more than this. When you rid the ego based way of living you then no longer require your mantras of affirmation. You will have no need to convince yourself that you are love. When you dismantle and dissolve ego you then believe who you truly are and you live from this place called love and stillness or you. To be truly still is to be consciously aware without any form of thought of being still.

As previously stated and in review, eventually your energy will not support negative ideas because the Law of Attraction will refuse to magnetize these ideas back to you. The universe will not give you what is untrue as the high vibration of the planet will not support this illusion and untruth. It is being revealed here that there will come a time when the Law of Attraction will no longer attract back to individuals ego based thoughts, ideas, opinions and old pain filled story emotions. It will only reflect or mirror back to you positive, high vibration thoughts, feelings and ideas. Presently the Law of Attraction mirror reflects everything you think, feel and believe and all comes back to you because you are sending this out to the universe and the universe is saying, "We will give this to you since this is what you are requesting." However, a point in energy is arriving when if you allow yourself to think a negative thought, idea or opinion it will not be mirrored or reflected back to you since the universal energy vibration is so high that it can not vibrationally or energetically send it back to you anymore.

As each individual awakens to their Spirit self and loosens the belief and allowances of ego this then raises the energetic vibration upon the entire planet. Much like a singular kiss of the butterfly wing upon the cheek of the wind's energy influences the entire planet. These truly are incredible times to be alive.

Dismantling Language

Dismantling Old Words – Forming New Words from an Energetic Vibration

When you hear language from others pay attention to your feelings. Words have energetic vibrations such as the word love, which will feel lighter than the word anger. This energetic vibration creates a feeling. Keep in mind or in thought what the word is meaning and recognize how this feels. When you read the following words or state them out loud, how do you feel, what is the energetic or vibrational charge?

1. Love

2. Joy

3. Fear

4. Peace

5. Anger

6. Stuck

7. Confusion

8. Transition

9. Spirit

10. Addiction

11. Darkness

12. I can

13. I can't

14. Allow

15. Star dust

16. Negativity

17. Stillness

18. I'm not enough

19. I am enough

20. Tough

21. Beauty

22. Easy

23. Sunrise

24. Sparkle

25. Happiness

How did you feel? How did your energy and physical body react when you read these above words and little phrases? Do the words feel light, soft, easy or heavy? It is here within the energetic vibrational weight where you discover what words you should and should not be using. For example, when you say the word love and feel the energy of this word, what does it feel like? Do you feel warm, light, gentle, peace-filled? Now say the word fear, what does this feel like? Do you feel a tightening in your heart and/or stomach area, a heaviness, coldness, do you perhaps experience a shortness of breath? Do the words in this list connect to ego or love? *In other words* are they ego based terminologies or love based language? Ego is a conceptual terminology placed in language, but love is the language of the heart. These are two different feelings, energies and vibrations.

As the recognition that ego is an illusion and is no longer welcome then every single everything wrapped around ego; all ideas, thoughts and opinions will dismantle, including its terminology. When you have shifted out of ego beliefs, the ego terminologies will no longer have an energetic charge for you and become benign rather than cancerous.

Even the word karma will leave our language, as well as past lives since you will no longer need to regress back into a past life for explanations because you won't require any explanations anymore. Therefore the dismantling of explanations, knowledge or information is presently occurring, leaving nothing. Nothing, defined as simplicity, vastness, emptiness, no explanations, no language of pain and no questions of why.

As stated previously in another chapter, affirmations such as, "I am love, I am grace and I am peace" will no longer be necessary to state since you will recognize your truth of knowing that you are love, peace and grace. Thus thinking will be alleviated, leaving only heart feelings.

What does all this mean? Language will weaken its hold and feeling everything will strengthen its hold or muscle. To feel everything and be present in this now feeling, actually has *no language* to describe itself. The new words emerging are words that are vibrations with no thoughts or verbal language. They will resonate with who you truly are, which is Spirit. Silence has its own speaking energy or language which has *no thing*.

Dismantling a Collection of Old Ideas

You are living during a time when the dismantling of old ideas will come forward for you to relinquish all that which is no longer necessary. One idea that will be dismantled is the thought of ***separateness***. You may think that you have been separate from others through depression, poverty, wealth, loneliness, fear and abandonment. This is false and you need to reconsider that what you are believing to be real may in fact not be real at all. Furthermore, society tries to convince you to buy this item, do this activity, achieve, be successful, say these words and if you aren't doing this, doing that, believing this, believing that, then of course you are separate and you need to be the same.

If you desire to be different, unique and special then are you still indicating to the world that you are separate? Yes, of course, but within your yearning of separateness you discover that you in fact feel that you don't belong and therefore separate yourself through a mask of stating, "I am unique and different from everybody – I am an inventor." But what you are really saying is the following, "I want to be my authentic self and this is being separate from those who are not being their true authentic selves." But does this necessarily mean you are then separating yourself from others? Yes and no, for example, you may believe that you are so authentic, real and true that you actually separate yourself from others and eventually begin to not enjoy your uniqueness because you may become angry within your own separateness by saying the following to others, "Don't you get what is going on here on the planet? The belly of the Mother Earth and the heart of Father Sky are in need of healing?" If you say this in anger to people who are not understanding then they will not listen to you as you are separating yourself as one with more knowledge, more information or in other words ego based and therefore you separate!

Anything that is ego based you have immediately separated or pushed yourself away from love or from yourself. So what to do? Let's dismantle and dissolve this into one more layer. If you feel separate and unique from others you may be still believing your old story of abandonment. When you are living through the emotions and beliefs of abandonment, then even if you feel and believe you are living your authentic self, you will create and attract separateness and abandonment. Ego will slip in and try to manage your system and build or grow your belief in separateness.

Be gentle upon yourself, allow your authentic self to emerge from the love within you, from your passion, not from wanting to be separate. This *wantingness* or desire is this: you are not feeling belonging due to possible old abandonment stories and you are just confirming this at a conscious level or subconscious/unconscious level. When you state you are different or more unique than others be careful, since this may indeed be ego convincing you that you are somehow more special than others because you are now living your authentic self. Be aware of this kind of idea, concept or emotion.

As you can see it is vital to dismantle this old idea of separateness. Being separate means ego and watch out for this since the ego will try to convince you that you aren't worthy nor are you living how others live. Certainly you may have some different ideas than other individuals, but this doesn't mean you are separate. Sure you may decide to dye your hair white or purple and wear pink shoes, but this doesn't make you separate, you are just you! Just be you! If you wish to colour your hair white or purple then do so as this is what you feel you would like to do for you. Not to live and relive your story of "I'm different, nobody understands me, nobody gets me, I am unique." This is separation and anger.

The more you live who you are the less separate you believe you are, as you then realize that everybody who has shifted into living their authentic selves are also wearing pink or polka dot shoes. You are living during a time where all people are moving into their own authentic selves. When you sojourn into your authentic self be careful that you aren't sabotaging yourself by believing and feeling you are different and special since all people are as *is*, all people are Spirit. Not separate, not uniquely separate just "*uniquely is*," "*isness*" is the Spirit in each, and how you express your isness is your uniqueness.

In fact, at some point in your awakening you may recognize and realize that even the term authentic will be dismantled as it too causes judgement. Meaning, pay attention to when you say to another person, "Look at me and my unique authentic self," or "Clearly *you* are not living your unique authentic self, like me." There is no authentic or inauthentic self – just is! If you wish to use the term authentic then know, believe and allow yourself to live each authentic moment fully. Even if you are living through depression, it still means you are living authentically in that moment until you move, shift and live the next moment. Each moment is perfectly connected to the next moment, authentically or as best as you know how in that now moment.

Another idea that is being further dismantled and dissolved is *coincidence*: the idea of coincidences have been focused, talked about and studied for a number of years. Many individuals believed the old ego idea that coincidences were random acts, no coinciding, no reason or perfection, just random. The dismantling of coincidence happened many years ago when the term coincide was broken into *co-incide* meaning everything coincides with everything. This term was then replaced with synchronicities, which means all in perfect time and reason. For example, if you were thinking about an old friend, whom you haven't heard from in many years, telephone calls you at the exact moment you were thinking about him or her, you would call this a synchronized event. Perhaps one or two or even more of these events happened throughout your day. What is being revealed now is that every single millisecond of your day is synchronized to the next single millisecond. This means you are synchronicity! You are a being of synchronicity and who you are is what you create in your life. You are the Creator, The One, The Being, this is you. Therefore, there is no co-creating because you are the Creator.

Create your life as if you were on a holiday and travel *in-joy*. Why would you be angry or *in-anger* on a holiday? Every single day should be a holiday, but the ego wants you to believe otherwise. It wants you to believe that you need a break, are worn out, and are burnt out! This is ego talking. If you believe the idea that you are burnt out then this is what you create. If you believe that you aren't burnt out, then you aren't burnt out. What do you wish to believe?

Have you believed a sequence of thought patterns for a number of weeks, months or years convincing you to not take care of yourself, sleep or eat well, to be angry, and to dislike your job? If yes, then of course you will believe that you are burnt out and now need to get away for a holiday. Once again dismantling of the ego is taking place here in this idea because what one needs to allow oneself to do is change their attitude about work, just change this way of thinking and see what happens.

Dismantle the ego based thoughts and live your life as a holiday, which means rest, peace and relaxation. Do you wait until the weekend or day off to rest and find peace? Meanwhile it is already inside of you. Even if you breathe deeply at your work desk or the assembly line or before you get up to teach a school lesson, just breathe and relax. Tell yourself to relax and you will. What will happen is that part of your self awakens since you are now allowing this awakening. You don't need to hold your breath until the weekend or your day off. What happens is we hear ego thoughts and forget about our breath. How often have you caught yourself not paying attention to your breath, but you still hear your thoughts of worry.

Breathe deeply and move into the stillness of who you are one millisecond by one millisecond, every day. Perhaps you would enjoy taking a yoga or meditation class. What you will eventually discover is that you are meditation and in fact you won't need to even take a class as you become aware that you are already a walking stillness or walking meditation. You are meditation or stillness with a pair of legs, you don't need to seek anything external of yourself to discover yourself.

You don't even need to learn to love yourself since you are love already. Perhaps you say the mantra, "I love myself, I am love, I am loved." This is just confirming who you are already and is bringing a deeper awareness into yourself. You are love and in fact you don't even have to read a book about how to attain love since it is you. Bring awareness into this soft belly part of who you are and you will begin to know that *you are your own guru*, the collective consciousness or The Being. Leave all that you don't need behind you. What you don't understand you don't need to understand, move forward in your knowing. The ego wants intellectual mindful explanations and understanding, but this is no longer necessary because there are no understanding's or reasoning's in love, in Spirit and in grace.

Knowing is just *knowing*, which is a feeling or an intuition. One day you may not understand why you need to follow a particular knowing. The ego wants to know the unknown and often times you hear people say, "I want to know the unknown because I am afraid of the unknown." Well, the unknown is already known and the following of your knowing already has set-up further knowing's and you don't need to worry. Just trust and allow the energy of faith to rest inside you. The idea that you are afraid of the unknown needs to be dismantled and dissolved from your belief system.

The idea that there are expectations is also being dismantled which means there are no expectations and everything is already here. Everything is all ready, all of your dreams and wishes are all ready here and waiting. You created these before you arrived in human form. They are already manifested so the unknown is impossible. One just needs to deeply follow his/her knowing or intuition and just be.

Have you ever noticed how squirrels dive from tree to tree in faith and know that they will find the next branch, stick or twig? If they do fall, the belly of Mother Earth simply bounces them back up onto the trunk of the tree and away they go again into their dance upon the branches. They just intuitively and instinctively know that the Mother's belly of nurturing is always there ready to catch them in her loving and All Knowing arms. This is the squirrel's food: love, trust, faith and knowing. This is what allows them to live and eat their physical food.

Without this instinctive knowing where would their freedom be? You too are a squirrel with a built-in food system of love, trust, faith, freedom and knowing. Just know that even if you fall upon the belly of Mother Earth she will bounce you back up to your feet in order for you to keep going. How amazing. All in perfect order – just know this!

Dismantling Time

T he idea of time is dismantling and slowly transitioning to being obsolete. Time is just simply illusion and as it dismantles, peace and *ease-ness* will fill these empty spaces of time and what you discover is that your thought of time has tried to cover your true self of peace and ease-ness.

Time is perhaps ego attempting to create more fear. There is never "a not on time event" and when you feel and know this then you will truly see what is going on. For example, if you are believing that you are late then you will be late, but perhaps you ended up in a traffic jam for some very specific reason to slow you and others down to a halt! When you arrive to where you are going you are in perfect Godly time or Spirit time and nothing more or less than this. If you explore your day you begin to realize that you may spend portions of it in fear, worry and anxiety. You now need to cease this and when you do, you will *increase your time* since there would be more time to spend on grace and peace or just being you. When you begin to believe that time is illusion you come to recognize there is a lot of time because the now moment, when expanded, presents to you the vastness of nows or all. Living out of time means being in the now, which has no time. When you live from patience you feel time stopping and then know there is no time. Fear, pain and suffering constrict and swallow-up space leaving you breathing shallow, feeling knots of fear, aches and more, all mixed within this illusion.

There is no time and the existence of time is of no time, and maintains itself steadfast and/or dominant amongst the illusion of fear. Without fear there actually is no time, but for some individuals they believe that without time there is fear, at least for those who live under the illusion of time. For those who are fearless, then time does not exist. If you live from a place of fear then you are living in a space that is filled with old thoughts, emotions and behaviour patterns. When free of the illusion or believe time is an illusion everything falls into place.

When you have arrived in a space of absolute rest and glory, you then arrive in a place of contemplation or the deepness of stillness. This place of contemplation is a grand place of being; it is the Oneness, the timeliness, the Infinity One, the endless and eternal. It is the recognition that time is illusion and is just a feeling. The ego can not reason with the intellectual idea that time is an illusion and will try to spin the intellect in circles. Yet the messages streaming through these words and sentences in this chapter about time are placed for you to *feel* that time is illusion and to stop your worry, anxiety and stress-filled thoughts and begin to allow your self to step forward in this day as Love.

Live under the illusion of time or believe time is an illusion.

These surely are some interesting times within this time of timelessness. It is now a time to organize your life in order for you to become filled with the feeling of *silent timelessness*. This means you just shift and flow in and out of timelessness silently, in peace and knowing all is perfect. Therefore your day is such that you move and flow with your feelings not your intellect, then as you do, you notice and feel each and every millisecond fully. You feel it is time to eat, sleep, walk or play and you flow into time which transforms into intuition.

Intuition could be called time instead of the clock time since when you feel your intuition you are then feeling time by saying, "I feel I would enjoy a walk now," "I feel I need to eat," "I feel I would like to go back to school," "I feel I would like to listen to some easy gentle music." Rather than stating, "It is time to go for a walk," "It is time to eat" or "It is time to sleep." Language is being split and reorganized here in order for you to think, feel and reshuffle what time is to you and how ego is involved.

When feeling your intuition you are living from Spirit and Spirit knows no time. Therefore you flow as Spirit moves and reshapes your day through feeling and knowing, thus timelessness. Remember too, dear reader, you are living during The Age of Aquarius or the flow of water. Primarily you are made of water, so flow with your natural essence or Essence.

As you practice timelessness more deeply you are able to move into the flow of your intuition. You also create and attract the *sense of your own intuition*, meaning you create your own feedback or intuitive sense. You sense the vibrational intuition through the Law of Attraction and create, hear and sense what is within you in order to shift the value of time. What this means is that the level of vibration that you live from is what you attract, which is what you sense through your intuition. For example, if your intuition is calling you to, "Speak to this person kindly, not in anger" but you don't and you only speak in anger then the level of vibration will attract the same level of vibration back to you, which is anger. However, if you do listen to your deepest intuition of love and speak only in kindness, then this will be returned and more of this will arrive thus carrying you more deeply into your intuitive self. Your intuitive self is always within you and is never opened by intellect. Intuition is so vast it can not answer an intellectual question. Time is an intellectual concept, intuition is a feeling and a knowing.

Perhaps you have heard, *time is of the essence*, which could now mean that sense is a place and the *essence* is the beauty of the flow of intuition. Therefore turn this around and say *intuition is an essence or a sense*. There are several terms or words that need to be used that are a higher vibration and greater strength in Spirit. Continue along the essence or sense line of eternal existence which is timelessness and results from the following *time lessons*:

Time Lessons

1. You ***recreate*** your life as you recognize you are love, perfect, whole and complete, All Ready without any form of time.

2. You ***allow*** transitioning, shifting and re-shifting throughout your entire life, all in perfect plan and order, and alignment.

3. You ***realize*** that you can live in an atmosphere or an arrangement created by yourself through vibration or a feeling of silent timelessness. This means to flow or flowing through your intuition in peace and a quiet harmonious knowing.

All energy doors open for you when you live
from your intuitive timeless self.

Dismantling the Therapeutic Process

L ove creates stillness and this stillness manifests itself in each person as a *solidity of stillness*. Pain and suffering creates misconceptions, misleadings and misguidance with no stillness. This is not who you are! Many people are believing they have a story and the ego loves this story of suffering and pain. However, these stories no longer need to exist in this present now moment. The belief that you are not your story is the truth. Do not allow others to convince you that your story is who you are. Therapists and counsellors who try to tell you that you need to review and dissect your story are missing a truth.

Sure maybe you have imprints of past life time influences, but only if you still believe this to be true. If you believe this to be true all you need to do is recognize the connection of some of your present day thoughts and behaviours to a past life time situation and once recognized, all will dissolve. You don't need fifteen years, or even one full year of therapeutic intervention to release the pain since all pain will literally drip away, when you recognize it. It may, at this point for you, seem unimaginable, magic, or even surreal, however the energies are now available upon the planet for *this* to happen, just allow. This therapeutic change is already attainable, real and will place a whole new perspective and an *interruption point* upon all therapeutic processes.

This interruption point is a point of awareness that the traditional therapeutic process is being dissolved and what is left is truth. The truth that your old childhood story of pain no longer needs to be spoken about over and over again for several months or even years. It just needs to be revealed, exposed then immediately released. The new energies within the planetary shift of today holds this revealing, exposing and releasing in its arms of love. Therefore an immediate understanding that you are no longer a victim and need to clutch to your childhood story as a crutch becomes recognized. The old story becomes an illusion because it has already happened, it's done and over. If you hold onto its perceived pain then you are clutching onto its illusion. The ego wishes for you to be in pain and suffering and to not release that which creates revenge, bitterness and victimization. In fact, when in pain often times you are unable to move and are forced into being still which leads you to see into and through the pain and then feel it as a teacher. When living *here* as the student you are being strongly encouraged to recognize that you are stillness and can now move (walk, talk, breathe) as stillness or a walking meditation.

It is a time when the view from the formed world to Spirit world will be so thin that retrieving memories of any childhood trauma will no longer need to occur. Just the recognition of this trauma will be only what is necessary since the higher conscious level of the nature of the universal energies will immediately clear, heal and reconfigure you. As the conscious level of individuals increases, then the number of childhood trauma cases will decrease.

You now no longer need to hold pain from your old story. Perhaps you are thirty-seven years old still clutching your thirty year old childhood story of pain and now it is time to release. Therefore the traditional psychotherapy and psychiatric processing will change and no longer value nor encourage ego to speak of blame and punishment for weeks, months and years. The new therapeutic process will be to assist people as they transition and become aware and filled with bliss and truth of self. Yes, release the old story but truly let it go so that you can feel who you truth*fully* are, which is peace and stillness.

Dismantling Life's Next
Steps Based on Fear

I t is a time to increase your awareness to eat properly, exercise, begin your own personal spiritual practice, and realize that you are One with everyone. What you say or do to others is just you doing this to yourself as we are all connected. There is a new consciousness here on the planet and this energy is shifting everybody into realizing that all are grace and that ego is no longer relevant and is illusion.

This new energetic consciousness is also indicating that one needs to move forward in life, take that next step but make this step not from fear, but love. What does this step look or feel like? How do you know this step is influenced by fear or love? The feeling of love is soft and it is your intuition or your intuitive self. Yet fear is prickly, hard, heavy and pushy. Your intuitive self is a tender yet strong, gentle yet deeply knowing and filled with Spiritual Oneness of the grander One.

The old belief system of feeling a decision through, then thinking about the decision, then feeling it through again and making a list of pros and cons, then talking to all of your friends is being dismantled as this process is wrapped around doubt, worry, fear, uncertainty. Now what is transpiring is to feel immediately your intuitive self and listen to your next step and do it immediately with no doubts, questions or concerns. What needs to be understood and felt is that everything is patiently waiting just for you. What you have been trying to manifest *is already manifested* even before you arrived in the human form, therefore the unmanifested is already manifested. The Being of who you are is already at work and the ego wants to stop you from Your Being's work and choose the path of fear, anger and resentment. What stops you is false fears. The future is all ready here, it isn't over there, but All Ready and available now. Future means a line of nows that have been created by one now after another now, each synchronized to the next now as designed by you. As you ask yourself the below questions, pay attention to how you feel and what you think.

What would you rather be doing right now?
Are you afraid of something?

The Being is The One Creator, Force, Source, You! You created your life before you arrived and now you choose which way to step. You could choose the way of fear or the way of joy and trust. Trusting that when you jump into a decision from truth and honesty then truth and honesty will be attracted back to you. Play to the edges and feel and see what happens. If you begin to follow your intuitive self, this will lead you to what is already manifested for you. This manifested way of being includes all forms of abundance. However, if you think you lack something and believe that abundance will fill up this space of lack, you then believe an ego based concept. The ego will try to convince you that abundance insinuates lack of something that you require in order to feel whole.

Just Be! Just be still as that is all you need to do.

"Do exactly what your 'yeah-but' says you shouldn't. Write that novel. Adopt a puppy. Keep the 'yeah' and kick the 'but'!"

Martha Beck (life coach)

Dismantling Religion

The next dismantling describes how some religion and religious ideologies or theologies are shifting out of ego into grace. The words of ego or the terminology associated with ego are also based within some forms and structures of churches and religious organizations. For example, the religious idea, for some, that if you don't believe in God, the external, you will not go to heaven and will surely die in hell, this is ego and fear based. At times a religion may base its teachings upon fear and scare its adherents into believing something that will save them. The dismantling of this is occurring now and more dismantling and dissolving will occur throughout these upcoming number of years as people awaken to who they truly are.

Beings of Light, with no fear.
Beings of Love, with no fear.
Beings of Joy, with no fear.

The ego wants you to believe that God, love and happiness are external of yourself and not within, since ego can not feel your inner Spirit. It wants you to seek external of yourself and to tell others that it is external. The God, the White Light, the love, the joy, the inner peace is who you are already. Nobody and nothing can ever take this away from you even if you believe that life is external of yourself in a God form, you still will be God inside of yourself. If you pray to an external God by saying, "Dear God" you are still praying with yourself **to** your higher self as you are God. Other terms for God could be White Light, Source and Essence. It really doesn't matter what term you use.

The ego also needs you to continually pray for items as it wants you to believe that you will be happier when you have objects of material wealth. Are you praying for something to satisfy a need which then says that you are believing in needing, which is also ego based? Meaning, you don't have enough and need more which the ego grabs hold of and feeds upon this form of energy as needing means pain. Needs and needing are under the misunderstanding of illusion. What needs are you believing that you have? The ego would have you believe that you are in constant need and require lots of everything to feel good. Stay present in your now moment and feel what is going on inside. You already have everything that you need in this now moment. If you do participate in a religious organization be aware of your inner self and feelings. Pray in peace and know all is exactly where it is suppose to be.

Dismantling Government

This next dismantling occurs at all levels of government and/or corporate management systems or the governing of countries. Ego has been allowed to be a large part of this and now is the time you will see more dismantling occurring as people come forth and request peace. The breaking down of all systems, which have been governed or ruled by ego, including countries, states, provinces and cities is now happening.

However, the dismantling of old ideas, thoughts, beliefs and allowances needs to start with self first. Once you are able to observe your own self, then you are able to see or observe and feel external of your singular One self to others, your own city, or village, country. Then to stand up in the strength of peace and grace, not of egoic fear or anger, but of love. You begin to see and feel everything differently. You recognize and clearly know that war is no longer acceptable. But this begins with you! You are the beginning of your Movement of Stillness and peace by moving your life in and only in stillness and realizing that you are this already.

Remember clearly that **you are The Creator**, not co-creating with a large God with a white bearded Santa Claus in the sky. You are the one who is creating, as is everyone else on the planet. So for reference, the statement made in the last chapter that if you pray to an external God you are still praying or meditating to you and for you and within you as God, you are the tree, bird, rock, whale, you are ALL. When you gaze at the sunrise and view its beauty of colour, shape, design and texture you feel it since it is you. When you say, "How amazing, how beautiful" you are speaking about you. The dismantling occurs for you when you realize that you are not separate from that sunrise and that you *are* the sunrise. You are One with everything and everybody. ALL people!

When you feel and know this to be true you then engage in standing forth for all people for peace, ease, love, stillness and truth. Many people have gathered already and continue to gather to say this needs to change as we can no longer live as war, hatred and untruths, it is now time to shift and change. The new energies of ego dismantling is now in ***deep motion*** and moving the ego out, so be aware and be still as the dismantling and dissolving occurs. Surrender and just let go!

Dismantling the Idea of Being Stuck

Perhaps you are presently believing that you are stuck and uncertain because the ego is saying to you, "You are stuck, stagnant and unhappy and not even sure what your favourite colour is anymore." This term stuck is no longer appropriate as it insinuates that you are in a deep sinking muck puddle and going nowhere. Perhaps you are feeling lost and uncertain of what you want in life, but realize you have actually entered into a beautiful *still point of existence*. You are not stuck as the ego declares, you are placed in a *point of stillness*. It is a place or space where you can make a decision to move forward. Perhaps you need to be in this space to be still and just sit, relax, slowly, gently, feel your next move or baby step in life.

Do not be hard on yourself and feel that you are stuck. You see how language can contaminate your thoughts and affect your life. Therefore if you feel and believe that you are just simply placed in a still point, this then releases the pressure to move forward quickly. When you relax and step out of the idea of being stuck and shift into existing in *ease*, within ease or the easiness of existing you feel, hear, taste, touch and smell your intuition at a very deep level. Plus, you then shift and take that one little step in ease, even if you can't feel this first little step just make a step, any step forward and believe and know this step is moving you forward. When you do this, the energy doors open and provide further ideas for your next step. This is how the universe works. Every single step you take, no matter how big or small, is allowing you to open the next door and the universe will say, "Here is the door and you just need to open it and walk across the threshold."

Your steps can change your reality of life. For example, if you feel that your first step is to go for a walk, and as you are walking you may: feel your next life step, meet somebody along the walking path who has a strong message for you, you may see something or realize something. Just take that one step and know that this step may change your entire outlook and perspective on life. The ego doesn't want you to move ahead, it wants you to believe you are stuck in a rut with no passion or direction. *This is illusion*.

Why allow ego to grab hold of your mind and thoughts? It is a time when many individuals are asking for meaning and purpose. There is no right or wrong step, only ***step***, and if you believe it will be the right step, then you have created conflict of right and wrong. In a twinkle of an eye this step could change your entire way of living, even if it is a walk outside and who knows what could happen? Just know you need to go for a walk and believe in yourself and trust yourself.

The concept or belief that the right path versus the wrong path is now illusion. You may ask, "But isn't war wrong?" The answer ***now*** is to be aware of the war, feel the pain and release these feelings and begin to bring Light into the situation and become consciously aware of what is happening. War begins with one person believing in pain, fear, anger, right, wrong, conflict, wanting power and control. In other words, they are believing in the illusion of ego and are now manifesting this illusion. Again, what you believe and who you are is what you will attract.

Ask yourself, "What are my dreams and wishes?" Begin to feel these out and say to the Universe or to yourself what you wish for. The universe will provide for you. Let go of ego beliefs of fears, which may be fears of failure or even success. The dismantling of ego is happening everywhere and this includes taking fear out of your dreams and wishes. Step into these dreams and know, believe and allow them to be true and you then realize they are already true.

Everything you create was once imagined and those who live a self-actualized way of living do not ever have any form of negativity or self doubt. They just know their dreams and wishes are here already and are aligned with them. Believe and know you are in perfect balance and have the capacity to absorb the fullest of life. This fullness is what the ego doesn't want you to believe you are already. You are already free and full and no longer need to read a book or take a course on this. You are a walking abundance!

Even if you don't have enough money for food for your family just Know, Believe and Allow yourself to trust that everything is in perfection. Trust that you will be provided for and are all ready being provided for in this now moment, just believe. Eventually you will begin to recognize that ***abundance*** means ***all***. In fact everything, all things were all ready ordered by you and for you before you squeezed into your human form.

As you move forward in life as a person of love and realizing the ego is fear, suffering and illusion, then many doors will open up for you. You truly begin to realize the falsehood of the ego and that it is a figment of your imagination, which is a thought you have allowed into your mind. This figment is only imagined, but yet creates the actual figment. The statement "ego is a figment of your imagination" could mean that if you even think of it as a figment, makes it real. Just by using the terms ***ego is an illusion*** still makes it real. Therefore, the completion of the dismantling of ego has occurred when the language and terminology defining anything about the ego dissolves and no longer exists (read more details about language within the Dismantling of Language section). These are most exciting times upon the planet to embrace everything and everyone.

Dismantling Feminine
and Masculine Ideas

T his next ego dismantling discussion will address the energies and roles of the feminine and masculine. You may be hearing and reading that the feminine energy is rapidly emerging upon the planet. More women are accepting leadership roles and there is information exposed that the energies of certain land formations are being transitioned from masculine energy to feminine. Or is this all illusion and then if it is illusion, what is truly happening? Are females more peaceful, nurturing and harmony-oriented than males? Has the ego entered into the definition of the roles of masculine and feminine and has this definition solidified itself for hundreds of years in many cultures? Is masculine really male and is feminine then female? Is there a feminine soft self moving throughout the planet and if so what exactly is this feminine? If you still believe that the softness defines only the feminine then the ego belief comes forth, but as ego dismantles, you will realize that all men and women are love and soft.

As the process of the dismantling of the ego continues this exposes the heart energies of: nurturing, caring, tenderness, softness, peace, joy, love and kindness, all of which have been defined as feminine. But heart energies are intertwined and thoroughly threaded within the cloth of both masculine and feminine. We are all the same, we are masculine, feminine, heart energies and Spirit. Heart energy has *always* in *all ways* been present upon the planet, but we as people have believed ego beliefs and allowed this untruth to reside in its illusion.

Let's dive more thoroughly into the idea of masculine and feminine. The ego has been defined through the male, but this now needs to be addressed as you enter into the deep energies of truth. When you are hearing that the planet is being transformed, re-shifted or reshuffled by the entry of the feminine energy be aware of what is being stated here. Are people implying that the male energy has no capacity to be heart and when in fact all people are heart, love, peace, Spirit and soul.

Perhaps the male has been so heavily programmed to believe in ego beliefs that this stereotype of male ego birthed itself through a collective belief system. This birthing resulted from several historical events backing up to early man. Boys within several societies have been taught to be tough, not to cry, don't be a girl and show your emotions. Is this ego teachings at work?

The male is now recognizing that it is time to begin to unfold their emotional softness and their true way of existing from deep within. This is what is happening upon the planet; the ego is dismantling and leaving feelings, softness, nurturing, grace and joy, which use to be considered as feminine. You will begin to realize that there is no masculine, feminine, male or female since we are *All One*. See and feel as all of us become connected, not as differences but as uni-sex, uni-verse, One-verse, One Unit, and One Song.

If you listen to the lyrics of the song *One Tribe* by The Black Eyed Peas the following words indicate we are one tribe, one blood and one planet:

One Tribe

"One world, one love, one passion ...
One tribe, one understanding ...
Cause where we gonna go is where we wanna be ...
The place where the little language is unity ..."

(The Black Eyed Peas. *The End*. Toronto,
Canada. Interscope Records. 2009.)

I would encourage you to listen to their song and feel their message of truth and promise. Not unlike John Lennon's lyrics in *Imagine* (Lennon, John. *Imagine*. California, USA. Capitol Records. 1989). John Lennon's lyrics message to us is to imagine a world with no separation, all hands joining and being One. Different times of musical composition but the same message, however, now is the time where you will hear more of the 1960's music coming forth because the message during that time was Oneness. Now is this time.

Dismantling of the Veil
Between Matter and Spirit

The term low vibration could be used to refer to any ego based language or situation. For example, when living in fear, anger, pain or suffering this is ego based and a lower vibration. The higher energetic vibrations are love, peace, joy and compassion. As previously stated in this book, polarities will no longer exist as a result of the emergence of the Oneness. In fact, when you reach a stage of recognizing you *are already* high vibration, and only this, then the low vibration or ego belief systems disappear. This recognition or remembering your true self will assist others into also recognizing they too are only higher vibration.

You can remember and feel this high vibrational energy when you are hiking in the forest, trekking up a mountain or swimming in the oceans and lakes. You feel wonderful as nature has no ego and is transparent in love. The human is the only one who is believing in ego and has created a form of pain. What is occurring however is this manifested ego pain is influencing nature through air, land and water pollution directed from us, resulting from our disrespect towards Mother Earth and Father Sky. The Mother and Father are now speaking and communicating to all people as they continue to cleanse and shift with the dismantling of ego, they too are part of the shift. It is time to stop the injury of the Mother and Father and to embrace them.

Realize too that the thinning of the energy veil is also happening. Meaning, the veil is thinning between the material heavy form and the spiritual form. You now have more access to Spirit and more individuals are speaking about Spirit and opening up to more possibilities. Which means more awareness of self, others, Mother Earth and Father Sky.

What has created this veil in the first place between matter and Spirit are people collectively believing ego teachings. However, separateness is sliding away in all areas of life and ego truly is being dissolved. The veil was created by you believing in ego illusions of fear, pain and suffering thus creating a self-protective veil. This blockage or veil is thinning in coordination with the dismantling of the ego.

As more individuals recognize and realize ego as illusion then the veil loosens its hold a little bit at a time and opens people up to further White Light possibilities. Thus, slowly shifting you closer to the luminated form of recognizing that everything stated by ego is false and you are just love. When living here we treat ourselves, others, Mother Earth and Father Sky with love, kindness and respect.

As stated earlier, presently upon the planet, ego resides in a perceived low vibration which is recorded as heavy. However, to stop this heaviness from fossilizing, you just need to recognize the ego right away. For example, if you are feeling betrayed in anyway, perhaps an affair in a relationship by your partner, then feel this pain of betrayal, release it and loosen its hold which rids the dust or the fluff of ego. The ego wants you to feel the pain of betrayal for years and to hold onto it and move into bitterness and revenge, thus fossilizing ego into your body, mind and emotion. This fossilization of ego may manifest itself as illness or dis-ease either physically, emotionally or mindfully. This may also create more illusions of triggers from old pain-filled stories of childhood where your mother or father were also betrayed through affairs. Then again is this a programmed unconscious thought you have carried with you as well? Which was manifested and a contributor to your personal veil of protection that states, "Nobody will ever get close to me again, ever!" However, if you read the section in this book titled Dismantling Old Stories you may come to realize that perhaps in your life contract you signed-up to experience betrayal, so all is in perfect plan and order.

Presently the ego is fizzing out as more people are coming to realize that it is illusion. The book entitled *Power Versus Force* by David Hawkins contains information about muscle testing, and calibrating energetic vibration. This book demonstrates how your energy tests stronger on higher vibrational foods, thoughts, music, books and more. Then in turn tests lower vibrationally on ego based fear thoughts. For example, your energy vibration tests very low on blame, fear, guilt and anger but higher in love, peace, joy and compassion. Since we are living during the dismantling of ego, this book entitled *Power Versus Force* and others will need to be rewritten as the lower vibrations will eventually not exist.

Energy workers will also see a shift in their practice because of the ego dismantling and will work more towards assisting clients to remember and know they *are already* high vibration. Therefore, the philosophies of healing energy work will shift through these dismantling times. The ego wants you to believe you are not well physically, emotionally and mindfully. It wants you to stay in pain and be here and not shift or move from this place of pain.

The ego doesn't want you to feel your intuitive Spirit-filled self. The intuitive self is who you are naturally, with a strong knowing, so much so you will no longer need to go and see a practitioner to get your answers as you begin to recognize that you know and feel all that you need. It is no longer necessary to use a pendulum, just feel inside of yourself, as all of the answers to your questions are there. Therefore when you arrive at this still place inside, you will know that you have experienced your intuitive self of joy, bliss, peace and you then shine through your form. Thus formless and recognizing your veil has thinned and released.

In addition, the planet or universe will no longer be identified as planet but a place of Origin. As you move into a place of living from Origin you begin to realize that you are the Universe. All is perfect! When the astronomer/physicist Galileo (1564 – 1642) studied the stars, moon, sun, and Milky Way he was able to recognize that everything was in perfect plan, order and absolute harmony. This term harmony means galaxy or Universe, which means Spirit and flow. It is here within the galaxy of life you discover the stars, moon, sun and Milky Way and you begin to realize that everything is perfectly placed and are now shifting with the shift of the planets' vibration and energy. It can't help but change and shift.

As the vibration increases upon the planet this affects the galaxy and its movement of stars, moon, sun, planets, Milky Way(s), and black holes. The harmony of the shifts affect the rhythm of the movement of everything. For example, the vibrational frequencies of the highest form vibrates at a very high, fast and fine energetic level. The rhythm created from this vibration sings the harmony of the universe and in particular, for these purposes, the galaxy.

The word Universe means uni-verse or one song and the harmony of the galaxy or universe is flowing up and down this bar line of music in perfect rhythmic timing. The galaxy is holding the Earth, Mars, Saturn and all planets and other dimensions in place. Without the galaxy you would not be grounded and would fall out of form into an ungrounded style of being which means your form would float on the ceiling and your whole self would be out-of-place and in-space. But why would this be such a troubling thought to experience no gravity within our galaxy? The galaxy *is* actually slowly shifting and changing and in fact the gravity's pull is becoming less intense and more in harmony with the vibration of what is occurring within each person. The gravity's pull is lessening its hold as each individual shifts into a higher vibrational attraction within their selves. This will not only resonate within oneself and others but will create a pull away from form and body. Therefore as the veil thins so does gravity.

Gravity is thinning but not at an enormous rate, just a gentle rate of shifting or moving. It is here within the shifting and moving whereby one is able to feel lighter and not so heavy. So does this mean that people will be floating on the ceiling shortly? No of course not since what this is indicating is more of an energetic experience rather than a physical experience. As you shift vibrationally the energy or the spiritual magnetic field places you upon the inner layer (which is the thinnest) of the force or pull of gravity and you are able to see all things more clearly and more substantially. You are able to recognize that as you shift into a new vibrational existence you then are able to see and feel everything so very differently. Then you realize and remember that you *are* of high vibration already and when this realization happens you begin to feel more energy, Spirit and vibration moving through your body or form. Thus, thinning of the veil or your body!

You are able to raise yourself above the planet and see it from a different point of view. You feel lighter and a Lightness of Being. As you allow yourself to float above the planet, visualize and feel all people holding hands outside of the Earth in the galaxy and surrounding the Earth in a large circle. It is here at this point in this visualization where you will feel the gravity's pull, but differently, and not such a heavy pull. This gravitational pull is subsiding slowly and efficiently. You will begin to feel that all are One, connected, heart, love and fine vibration. As more individuals remember, this then loosens the gravitational pull or the Law of Gravity.

Therefore the melding of *all* into beauty, peace, stillness, joy and love begins to happen. The Homo-Luminous form has no veil, no form, no ego, only love. This shifting or transforming is a natural and easy movement back to heart energy or home which is a place of comfort, peace, tranquility and ease. Actually, there is no language to describe this true awakening. This true awakening or ascension occurs when the parallel world of Spirit awakens to a different state of being and what this means is the following: the solid formed world thins and slides or melds into the Spirit world thus, *thinning of the veil*.

As the veil thins between Spirit and form, you then shift back to your original self. This is your transparent self or the Homo-Luminous formlessness which is a body of energy that is Spirit. Beautifully illustrated in *Sacred Mirrors*, Alex Grey captures the pure essence of all of us as the Homo-Luminous form/ formlessness (further description of Homo-Luminous see Glossary).

The planet and Spirit are shifting together as One and at some point all humans will indeed make that natural shift to be awakened to what's going on. The ego is being dismantled from everything slowly. It is as if a thin layer is collectively being removed, then another layer, then another layer of ego-based ideas. This is presently a slow movement in many areas of all civilizations. However, once one understands from a feeling perspective, then this *point of feeling* is the beginning of the awakening or remembering of who you are already.

Dismantling Ideas Relating to Food

The dismantling of the old ways of eating has arrived and you may want to re-examine your own way of eating. The questions asked here are: "Why eat fear? Why not eat love?" When you think and feel it that way you may then decide to not eat poison, but joy. One eats fear because you have been taught through old belief systems that this will make you feel better. Thus the ego at work trying to teach you that anything external of self will help you feel better as ego can not feel your Spirit. So next time you need to feel comfort, instead of eating fear eat love, try it out. Or don't eat and go for a walk, call a friend, do the opposite of what you would usually do and see how you feel.

Your feeling is the intuitive knowing, which is the part of you that has never left or changed. It is the part of you that says, "Don't eat that big bag of potato chips" or "Don't say that angry statement to the cashier." These are your intuitive knowing's messaging to you and all people, everybody has this knowing. Ego wants you to believe that you deserve to eat the large full bag of potato chips since they will give you comfort, which is really all wrapped around pain, suffering and fear. Deserving is no longer a word that reflects peace and actually means you are missing something. Deserving then may be interpreted as painful or suffering. Even if you have had a great day and you feel you deserve a big bag of potato chips to celebrate the day, how does this work then with ego? Perhaps you are having difficulty feeling celebratory within yourself and need a way of gratification external to your self.

Something to ponder: perhaps potato chips are good and healthy, and we have just been conditioned to believe they are not. What would happen if a break-through research revealed to the world that the healthiest form of food are potato chips. What would you do? Throw out all of your organic carrots, apples, oranges and stock up on potato chips because they are high in minerals, vitamins and good healthy fat? What would you believe? And what would be your action?

If your belief system is understanding that everything you eat is healthy and good in moderation not to extremes, then would you feel more peace"full"? Perhaps you believe that eating only certain foods is better than eating other forms of foods. Or perhaps you just eat potato chips all day long knowing they are actually gifting you all the nutrients you require. It then comes down to how you think about everything. If you believe that the ego is illusion then it is and this is how you live, believing and knowing there is only love. If you believe there is ego and it is a good thing, then this is how you will live. It is all based on your belief. But why would you believe in a destroying ego trying to convince you that it is not? Why would you eat potato chips when indeed they may destroy your cholesterol system and your physical form?

Here is the key! If you know the ego is illusion and it is out to destroy, then will you automatically stay away from its low vibrational energies? You will reach a point where you no longer want to live in pain and suffering. Then no matter what the ego says or tries, you simply laugh and send it away. If you pass by a big bag of potato chips and feel a craving for them, you ask the craving, "Why am I craving?" Feel the answer and make your decision. Maybe you laugh and purchase the bag, but eat a few chips at a time, not the whole bag and feel what your body feels like. If you are living from a total surrendered state of love, are you even attracted to the bag of potato chips?

When one has awakened to their true selves of love, peace and joy ***and*** you feel, believe and know the ego is illusion, then what happens is you automatically allow:

- Weight to drop off your physical form.
- Worries to dissolve and anxiety to loosen.
- Aging to slow down.
- Stress on your body to be released.
- Yourself to shine.
- Yourself to feel full and true.
- Yourself to not feel or believe you need something external of self to satisfy you in order to fill up that craving, since there will be no more craving.

> ***This is the start of an amazing life.***
> ***Have your daily intake of love energy,***
> ***not unlike vitamins.***

When you begin to catch ego thoughts and release them, you recognize that your energetic vibration increases and you begin to actually feel lighter. Then you realize that you are already high vibration and have allowed yourself to believe otherwise. This means you are changing and this is a wonderful change. You start to not like the taste of certain foods or drinks, and are not even attracted to them anymore. You begin to enjoy natural foods that have ***sunlight energy***, such as fruits and vegetables and drink more water. You attune yourself to your physical form and take better care of this vessel.

As the ego gets dismantled there is less thinking and more clarity, which means no thinking or blockages. This is The Age of Transparency and The Age of Aquarius, where everything is about White Light transparency or being crystal clear. Each person is made up of mainly water and within their water molecules are crystallized energetic particles.

The book *The Hidden Messages in Water*, by Masaru Emoto (Emoto, Masaru. *The Hidden Messages in Water*. California, USA. Hayhouse Publishing. 2005.) examined the actual water molecules of water droplets from a variety of water sources around the world. Emoto discovered that each of these molecules is different and the design of these molecules matches directly to the energetic vibration of the environment. In other words, in a country that has been through war and continues to create more war, the crystals or the designs of the water molecules are broken and not in the purest form or design.

The places where there is no war, the energetic vibration is high or finer in vibration, the molecules of the water as designed by the crystals, are in absolute perfect form. Each one of us have crystals within our water molecules in our body of cells. Therefore, you cannot live without the absorption of water or you will dry up your crystal molecules of the water crystals and surely perish. Meaning, your crystals will dry up, crackle and create a brittle way of being and this is defined by ego. Ego wants moisture out of your body and wants you to be stiff, raw and brittle. The natural creation of the crystallized water molecules are moist, fluid, crystal clear in high vibration and in the fullest of love.

Remember that water requires water and sunlight in order to maintain the crystal energies within your physical form and energy body. Plus, as the sun reflects upon the water and through the crystals this creates rainbow crystal healing energies, which are the new energies upon the planet. Eat foods that are naturally connected to the sun of all colours of the rainbow. You will notice recipe books on book store shelves about Rainbow Diets. It is time to begin to readjust your food intake and observe how your body feels and eat ***in-joy***.

Dismantling the Medical System

D ismantling and dissolving an ego belief system from the medical field will happen and this is already happening. Even medical language will shift and restructure. For example, there will come a time when you will no longer be told you have a certain number of years to live, due to an illness. This is all ego based power and control through the language and terminology stemming from the medical professional. The medical professional was trained to say words specifically because of medical obligations which may not come from grace, but from ego.

The ego wants you to believe that everything is not ok and not perfect. In fact, if you are experiencing disease then the ego wants you to feel pain, suffering and attach to fear, depression, revenge, anger and resentment. The ego belief system wants you to hold onto these negative feelings to create more of the same, dis-ease. Grace, which is who you truly are, wants you to feel love, peace, stillness and an absolute knowing that everything is ok and is in perfect plan and order, even an illness or dis-ease.

An illness or dis-ease is a teacher for you to recognize, observe and to realize who you truly are, which is love. It may be a time for you to be quiet, for you to look deeply within yourself and to feel the pain, and *release the pain*. The ego wants you to keep the pain and to wallow in being a victim instead of observing your life, feeling and releasing the pain and moving forward. Remember too that perhaps you chose to feel this pain in order to teach others about pain and how to gracefully release this pain in order to move into a still point of existence in your life. Perhaps you high-fived in energy form an agreement before you entered your present human body form to learn how to move through ego thoughts into grace, then to teach this to others through dis-ease.

Your body is a mirror reflection of your inner thoughts and beliefs. Every cell within your body responds to every single thought you think and every word you speak. You want to ease your thoughts (which may not even be your own thoughts) and not dis-ease the thoughts. Whenever you experience a negative thought be aware of this thought. All stress stems from resistance and in fact your entire body reacts from the directives of your mind, only if you elect it to. Your thoughts affect your health and therefore affect the planet. The moment you realize this, your identity shifts from ego to awareness.

As you become consciously aware of pain, it then grows because of the attention placed upon it, however, it then dismantles and dissolves because it's exposed. If you believe something to be true, it then becomes true for you. Why believe in pain and suffering when it doesn't exist, but only if you believe it to. There will come a time when you will not feel pain and suffering as it will no longer be necessary.

Presently the reason for the intensity of the pain and suffering is to bring people in recognition of ego. When pain and suffering are no longer necessary this then is when you realize that you are pure Spirit, love and joy and have shifted fully. When you realize this, you then begin to live from the *point of ending and beginning*, which is the only way to live. This is a point in your life when you realize that the end of something is the beginning. For example, if you have been diagnosed through the medical field with a dis-ease, but you *know* that this dis-ease is a great teacher for you, and you *know* that all is in perfect, plan and order. You also know that you are Spirit, then you have reached the point of ending old ideas and beginning new feelings and existing from ease and only ease. This ease of self already exists within you and you learn to shift and live from within your self.

Watch if you carry limited perspectives and beliefs. You may come to an awareness that everything you thought was true is no longer true. Spirit then pushes itself through your heart and you begin to shift your entire life as you gently and tenderly drop to your knees in openness. All is laid open to view. This is when you realize and feel freedom through Spirit and ***this*** feeling of freedom, fearless or loving kindness is who you really are. You then loosen the hold of disease and love yourself fully through ease. This is the place to be and within this space you actually live, breathe, allow yourself to come back to who you really are and to experience that which is you and all of you.

Ego wants you to believe that you are separate, dysfunctional, fearful, not good enough and filled with revenge. View the illustration below and examine how ego works in dis-ease through your belief system.

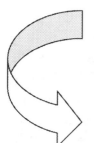

Ego = everything that appears to you as other or separate, not me.

- An exhausting frequency.
- This is called dis-ease.
- The cells bumping up against each other instead of flowing in harmony due to negative and judgemental thinking.

Are you attacking your true self? Are you believing you are something that you are not? Is this creating a fight or illusion inside of you? Stop this and loosen the hold of everything that appears to be negatively attached to your mind and awaken to who you truly are, please don't be afraid. There is nothing to fear, yet the ego will have you believe differently.

The ego no longer has a purpose. A very powerful statement speaks from the pages of the *Course in Miracles* (Schucman, Helen. *Course in Miracles*. Nebraska, USA. Published by Course in Miracles Society. 1976.) "All forms of sickness are physical expressions of the fear of awakening." The Course in Miracles also states that if we resist what is the natural flow of life, we waste energy and actually fight against ourselves.

When awakened, you realize you are enlightened already and just Light. Enlightened means to be Light and aware. If you are living a life of suffering, this is not being enlightened but unleavened. Unleavened, meaning squashed into a flat form or ego. Ego wants you to be flat upon the floor in depression and when you are unleavened you are living from the ego state of being. A place of constant fear and pain, physically and emotionally.

When living from a place of peace, one is able to heal oneself immediately by calling upon an energetic system known as self or Source. If you know you are Light, love, joy, peace or Source then allow yourself to be a vessel for the healing to move through you. Healing will occur in all forms. Language will heal as it moves through the person speaking to others or writing from a high vibrational place. Music will streamline through the musician to compose with ease. As each person increases his/her vibration or recognizes they are high vibration and are loosening the blockages or remembering, then the planet's vibration will also increase its frequency to assist all. Feel and know who you truly are, which is an open vessel for Light to shine through you to others to soften dis-ease and hold eachothers hands in glory.

Part IV

Final Message

*These are marvelous times to **be-living** upon the planet and **believing** in our planet and who we truly are, which is Spirit.*

A Gentle Conclusion

As you absorb and continue to reflect upon the messages that you have just read, know everything is in perfect plan and order. Perhaps you are presently experiencing a dismantling and dissolving of the ego in your life; just allow this to happen, let go and breathe into your stillness of being, which is the place or space of who you truly are. This dismantling is a gift to you, say thank you and allow *your self* to move more deeply into life. I read this quote from somewhere in my travels through books and feel that it captures the final essence of this book, as paraphrased:

"If you began to treat yourself with love, can you imagine all the change that would happen, just like magic, in your life? You would never be jealous of others. There is no way you could ever feel hate. Right away you would let go of any anger left in your mind against anyone who had ever hurt you. You wouldn't even have the need to forgive anyone, because there would be nothing to forgive. Your mind would be completely free, if love was moving through you ..."

You would then realize that you are just love and only this. Just imagine and know that now is a space or a place for people to realize it is time to be who you are now!

Peace and Happiness
Love
Is
Who You
Are
All Ready

Glossary

<u>All Ready or All Readiness</u> – Knowing that everything is in perfect plan and order. Everything is already done – just trust.

<u>Automatic Writing</u> – Allowing oneself to fully open to writing freely with no thought.

<u>Awakened</u> – When you realize you are Spirit first and foremost, but living a human experience. Realizing that you are peace and stillness already. You have nothing to achieve to be this stillness.

<u>Back Engineering</u> – Taking apart all pieces in order to re-construct or re-build in a better more efficient way.

<u>Calibrated Vibration</u> – The measuring of the vibration of energy, for example, fear is calibrated at 100 and love is 500.

<u>Channeling</u> – Streamlining information or being a vessel for the messages to move through you.

<u>Energy</u> – All have an energy system throughout their body and external of their body.

<u>Homo-Luminous Form</u> – This form has no ego. It is the formless Spirit of peace, joy, love and bliss.

<u>Homo-Sapien</u> – Human form relating to hunter and gatherer.

<u>Knowing</u> – That place inside you that is a deep believing of yourself. A true understanding without doubt.

<u>Meme</u> – A programmed thought that you believe to be true.

<u>Oneness</u> – All beings coming together as One Consciousness with the new Mayan calendar post-2012 representing the Oneness.

<u>Original Self</u> – Spirit is the original self, that whole part of self that is peace, love, joy, passion and compassion.

<u>Re-formation</u> – A new way of beginning to live your life.

Notes

The snail says to itself, "I will slowly move forward and begin my day by existing in my mobile home. I'll eat my daily food, walk my daily walk and be a role model for others. Even though I am little, I am filled with the Spirit of strength, purpose and meaning. Humans will watch me as I slowly flow with life and that I trust everything is in perfect order. Nothing is out of place."

Notes

"The easiest things are the most delicious!"

Suse Ives
(proprietor of Simply Tea and Chocolate)

Notes

"The greatest achievement was at first and for a time a dream. The oak sleeps in the acorn; the bird waits in the egg; and in the highest vision of the soul a waking angel stirs. Dreams are the seedlings of realities."

James Allen
(author)

Notes

"... and there, in the midst of the light, they saw the ends of the chains of heaven let down from above: for this light is the belt of heaven, and holds together the circle of the universe."

Plato

Notes

"The pursuit of truth and beauty is a sphere of activity in which we are permitted to remain children all our lives."

Albert Einstein

Notes

Walking in Beauty: Closing Prayer from the
Navajo Way Blessing Ceremony

"With Beauty before me may I walk.
With Beauty behind me may I walk.
With Beauty above me may I walk.
With Beauty below me may I walk.
With Beauty all around me may I walk.
With Beauty in me may I walk
As I walk the Beauty Way."

About the Author

Jacqui Derbecker is a consultant, speaker, author, clairvoyant, visionary and an education teacher. Through her passionate exploration of deeper consciousness, she teaches clients how to connect with their inner authentic self, enabling them to realize that they are the Essence of Spirit.

She channeled the book, *"Movement of Stillness – As Revealed In The New Mayan Calendar post-2012"* and an 80 card deck called *"The Know, Allow and Believe Healing Cards."*

She is the founder of the magazine *"Another View"* and The Waterview Space Centre, outside of Toronto, Ontario, Canada where she teaches classes, gives personal readings and consultations.

www.jacquiconsults.com
www.thewaterviewspace.com